NO WHEAT YES ALMOND FLOUR

Over 150 Top Healthy Low Carb Recipes To Bake Bread, Cakes, Cookies, Crackers And More Without Gluten

By

Olivia .T. Anderson

CONTENT

Introduction 3

What Makes Almond Flour Better Than Wheat Flour 4

How To Properly Store Almond Flour For An Extended Shelf Life 5

Want To Bake Perfectly With Almond Flour? Here Are Some Vital Tips 6

Step By Step Guide To Make Almond Flour At Home 7

ALMOND FLOUR BREAD RECIPES 9

ALMOND FLOUR CRACKERS 31

ALMOND FLOUR ENTREEES 34

ALMOND FLOUR PIE RECIPES 51

ALMOND FLOUR PASTRIES 57

ALMOND FLOUR CRUSTS 66

ALMOND FLOUR CAKES 74

ALMOND FLOUR CUPCAKES 83

ALMOND FLOUR COOKIES 91

ALMOND FLOUR BARS 100

Introduction

Dear baker, thanks for picking a copy of this book! This almond flour cookbook is for those looking for a wheat-free and gluten-free option for baking. It covers almost every category of baking ranging from breads, crackers, cakes, scones, pies, and so on!

The recipes in this cookbook are great to tryout, well detailed and each recipe provides valuable tips and recommendations such as customization options and recipe variations, all to make things more interesting.

Happy baking!

What Makes Almond Flour Better Than Wheat Flour

No doubt, wheat flour is the most popular for baking, however, this doesn't necessary means it's the best. There are other alternatives, and one of them is almond flour. If you are wondering why almond flour is better than wheat, here are some valid reasons:

1. Gluten-Free: this is one of the main reasons people are switching to almond flour for baking. As opposed to wheat, almond flour is naturally gluten-free, making it a suitable option for those with gluten sensitivities or celiac disease.

2. Low Carbohydrate Content: if you are on a low-carb diet or keto diet, then almond flour is a good substitute for wheat. This is because almond flour generally has a lower carbohydrate content compared to wheat flour.

3. High in Healthy Fats: Almond flour is rich in monounsaturated fats, which are considered heart-healthy. These fats may help improve cholesterol levels and provide a source of sustained energy.

4. Rich in Nutrients: now, it is not just about gluten, what about nutrients? Yes, Almond flour contains essential nutrients such as vitamin E, magnesium, and antioxidants which contribute to overall health and well-being. It also has a rich taste too!

5. Blood Sugar Control: Almond flour has a lower glycemic index compared to wheat flour. Foods with a lower glycemic index are digested more slowly, leading to a slower and steadier release of glucose into the bloodstream. This can be beneficial for managing blood sugar levels.

7. Dietary Fiber: Almond flour contains dietary fiber, which is important for digestive health. Fiber can help promote a feeling of fullness and support regular bowel movements.

How To Properly Store Almond Flour For An Extended Shelf Life

Notably, almond flour has a shelf life of 4-6 months when kept in the fridge. With that said, to extend the shelve life and preserve the quality of almond flour, here are some valuable things to do:

1. Use Air-Tight Container: Transfer almond flour to an airtight container or a resealable bag designed for food storage. This prevents exposure to air, moisture, and pests, which can cause the flour to spoil faster.

2. Store In A Cool, Dark Place: Store almond flour in a cool, dry place away from direct sunlight. Excessive heat and light can accelerate rancidity and degrade the quality of the flour.

3. Refrigeration or Freezing: Almond flour has natural oils that can go rancid over time. For longer-term storage, consider refrigerating or freezing it. If refrigerating, ensure it's in a tightly sealed container to prevent moisture absorption. When freezing, use a freezer-safe bag or container, and allow it to come to room temperature before using. As stated earlier, it can last 4-6 months when refrigerated, and about a year when frozen.

4. Labeling and Date: Label the container with the purchase or preparation date to track its freshness. Almond flour, when stored properly, can last for several months to a year.

5. Avoid Moisture: Moisture is an enemy to the shelf life of almond flour. As you plan to store, ensure the container and the utensils used are completely dry before transferring the flour. Any moisture can lead to clumping or spoilage.

6. Frequent Use: If you use almond flour infrequently, consider buying smaller quantities to ensure freshness. It's often better to purchase in smaller batches that you can use up within a reasonable time frame.

Want To Bake Perfectly With Almond Flour? Here Are Some Vital Tips

If you are new to baking with almond flour, you might be nervous not to make mistakes, but you need to relax! Chill, mistakes are part of the learning curves and help you become better. However, to reduce your mistakes and help you bake like a professional even at your first trial, here are some vital tips:

1. Measure Accurately: Almond flour is dense, so accurate measuring is crucial. Use a kitchen scale for the most precise results, as almond flour can easily compact in measuring cups.

2. Combine with Other Flours: Almond flour can be combined with other gluten-free flours like coconut flour or tapioca flour for better texture and structure in baked goods.

3. Use Binding Agents: Since almond flour lacks gluten, add binding agents like xanthan gum, eggs, or ground flaxseeds to help hold the ingredients together.

4. Adjust Liquid Content: Almond flour absorbs more moisture than regular flour. Adjust the liquid content in your recipe accordingly by adding a bit more liquid (like eggs, oil, or milk) to achieve the right consistency.

5. Add Leavening Agents: Incorporate baking powder or baking soda to help the baked goods rise, as almond flour can create denser textures without these agents.

6. Prevent Burning: Almond flour browns faster than wheat flour. Cover baked goods with foil halfway through baking to prevent over-browning.

7. Sift Almond Flour: Sifting almond flour can help break up any clumps and aerate it for a lighter texture in your baked goods.

8. Mix Well: Mix almond flour thoroughly with other dry ingredients to ensure even distribution in the batter or dough.

9. Chill Dough: For recipes like cookies or pie crusts, chilling the dough before baking can help them hold their shape better during the baking process.

Don't worry about these general tips because each and every recipe in this almond flour baking book comes with useful tips and step by step instructions tailored to the specific recipes, so be rest assured that things will turn out just fine!

Step By Step Guide To Make Almond Flour At Home

Well, you can buy readymade almond flour from stores or you can prepare it yourself at home.

Note that Homemade almond flour has a slightly different texture than store-bought varieties due to home equipment limitations, but it's equally versatile and great for various recipes. Whichever, choice you make, just know that baking with almond flour is exciting!

Even if you have bought from store, you can still try making it from scratch to know what it feels like. Now, here's how to make almond flour at home:

Equipment Needed:
1. Food Processor or High-Powered Blender
2. Fine-Mesh Sieve or Sifter
3. Measuring Cups

Steps:
1. Gather Ingredients and Equipment
Get raw, unsalted almonds. You can choose the quantity depending on how much almond flour you need.

2. Prepare Almonds
Measure out the amount of almonds you want to turn into flour. You can start with around 1 cup or more as needed.

3. Blanching (Optional)
To remove the almond skins for a finer flour, blanch the almonds. To do this, boil water and pour it over the almonds. Let them sit for about a minute, then drain and rinse them with cold water. Pat dry the almonds with a clean towel. The skins should slip off easily.

4. Dry Almonds (Optional)
Spread the almonds on a baking sheet and let them air dry for a few hours or bake them in a preheated oven at a low temperature (around 200°F or 95°C) for 15-20 minutes until they are dry but not browned. This step helps in getting a finer texture.

5. Grind Almonds
Place the almonds in a food processor or a high-powered blender. Pulse or blend the almonds in short bursts to avoid overheating. Stop periodically to scrape down the sides and ensure even grinding.

6. Sieve the Flour (Optional)
For a finer almond flour, sift the ground almonds through a fine-mesh sieve or flour sifter. Any larger pieces left behind can be reprocessed to achieve a finer texture.

7. Store Almond Flour
Store your homemade almond flour in an airtight container in a cool, dry place or in the refrigerator to maintain freshness. It can last for several months if stored properly.

Tips:
- Avoid over-processing: Almonds can turn into almond butter if processed for too long, so be attentive.
- Grinding smaller batches at a time yields a finer flour.
- Ensure the flour is completely dry before storing to prevent it from clumping or going rancid.

Now, let's start baking!

ALMOND FLOUR BREAD RECIPES

Try almond flour bread for a cozy, gluten-free option that's soft inside and crispy outside. Perfect with jams or as sandwich bread.

Basic almond flour bread

Preparation Time: 10 minutes **Baking Time:** 40-45 minutes

Ingredients:
- 2 cups almond flour
- 1/4 cup psyllium husk powder
- 1 teaspoon baking powder
- 1/2 teaspoon salt
- 4 eggs
- 1/4 cup olive oil or melted butter
- 1 tablespoon apple cider vinegar
- Optional: Seeds (like sesame, poppy, or sunflower) for topping

Directions:
1. Preheat your oven to 350°F (175°C). Grease or line a loaf pan with parchment paper.
2. In a large bowl, whisk together the almond flour, psyllium husk powder, baking powder, and salt until well combined.
3. In another bowl, beat the eggs. Add olive oil or melted butter and apple cider vinegar, whisking until well combined.
4. Pour the wet ingredients into the dry ingredients and mix until a thick dough forms.
5. Transfer the dough to the prepared loaf pan, smoothing out the top with a spatula.
6. Optional: Sprinkle seeds on top of the loaf for added texture.
7. Bake for 40-45 minutes or until the bread is golden brown and a toothpick inserted into the center comes out clean.
8. Remove the bread from the oven and let it cool in the pan for 10-15 minutes before transferring it to a wire rack to cool completely.

Important Notes:
- Psyllium husk powder helps give structure and acts as a binder in almond flour bread recipes.
- The bread may have a denser texture compared to traditional wheat bread due to the absence of gluten.
- Store almond flour bread in an airtight container in the refrigerator for up to a week or freeze slices for longer storage.

Nutritional Value:
approximately 150-200 calories, 12-15g of fat, 6-8g of protein, and 4-6g of carbohydrates per slice.

Almond Flour Sandwich Bread

Time to Prepare: 15 minutes **Cooking Time:** 40-45 minutes

Ingredients:
- 2 cups almond flour
- 1/4 cup coconut flour
- 1/4 cup psyllium husk powder
- 1 tsp baking powder
- 1/2 tsp salt
- 4 large eggs
- 1/4 cup melted butter or coconut oil
- 1/2 cup unsweetened almond milk
- 1 tbsp apple cider vinegar

Step by Step Directions:
1. Preheat your oven to 350°F (175°C). Grease a loaf pan and line it with parchment paper.
2. In a mixing bowl, combine almond flour, coconut flour, psyllium husk powder, baking powder, and salt.
3. In another bowl, whisk together eggs, melted butter or oil, almond milk, and apple cider vinegar.
4. Mix the wet ingredients into the dry ingredients until a smooth batter forms.
5. Pour the batter into the prepared loaf pan and smooth the top.
6. Bake for 40-45 minutes or until the bread is golden and a toothpick inserted into the center comes out clean.
7. Allow the bread to cool in the pan for 10 minutes, then transfer to a wire rack to cool completely before slicing.

Recipe Variations:
- Add herbs or seeds like rosemary, sesame seeds, or poppy seeds for added flavor.
- Incorporate grated cheese into the batter for a cheesy variation.

Topping Options:
- Spread butter or almond butter on slices.
- Use as a base for sandwiches or toast.

Customization Options:
- Experiment with different spices or seasoning blends for unique flavors.

Important Notes:
- Ensure all ingredients are at room temperature for best results.
- Store the bread in an airtight container in the refrigerator for up to a week.

Nutritional Value: (Per serving)
- Calories: 180 kcal
- Total Fat: 15g
- Carbohydrates: 6g
- Fiber: 3g
- Protein: 7g

Banana Bread

Preparation Time: 15 minutes **Cooking Time:** 50-60 minutes **Yield:** 1 loaf

Ingredients:
- 3 ripe bananas, mashed
- 2 eggs
- 1/3 cup melted butter or coconut oil
- 1/2 cup honey or maple syrup
- 1 teaspoon vanilla extract
- 1 3/4 cups almond flour
- 1 teaspoon baking soda
- 1/2 teaspoon cinnamon
- 1/4 teaspoon salt
- Optional: 1/2 cup chopped nuts or chocolate chips

Directions:

1. Preheat the oven to 350°F (175°C). Grease a loaf pan.
2. In a large bowl, mix mashed bananas, eggs, melted butter or oil, honey/maple syrup, and vanilla extract.
3. In another bowl, combine almond flour, baking soda, cinnamon, and salt.
4. Gradually add the dry ingredients to the wet ingredients, mixing until just combined.
5. Fold in chopped nuts or chocolate chips if desired.
6. Pour the batter into the prepared loaf pan.
7. Bake for 50-60 minutes or until a toothpick inserted into the center comes out clean.
8. Allow the bread to cool in the pan for 10 minutes before transferring to a wire rack to cool completely.

Recipe Variations:
- Add 1/2 cup shredded coconut or diced dried fruits for added texture.
- Substitute a portion of almond flour with coconut flour for a slightly different texture.
- Experiment with different spices like nutmeg or cloves for a unique flavor.

Topping Options:
- Spread with almond butter or cream cheese.
- Drizzle with honey or a glaze made of powdered sugar and almond milk.

Customization Options:
- Make it vegan by using flax eggs and vegan butter or coconut oil.
- Adjust sweetness by adding more or less honey/maple syrup based on preference.

Important Notes:
- Ensure bananas are ripe for optimal sweetness and flavor.
- Don't overmix the batter to avoid a dense texture.

Nutritional Value: (Per slice - serves 10)
- Calories: ~220
- Total Fat: 14g
- Carbohydrates: 22g
- Fiber: 3g
- Protein: 5g

Zucchini Bread

Preparation Time: 20 minutes **Cooking Time:** 45-55 minutes **Yield:** 1 loaf

Ingredients:
- 1 1/2 cups shredded zucchini (about 1 medium zucchini)
- 2 eggs
- 1/3 cup melted coconut oil or olive oil
- 1/2 cup honey or maple syrup
- 1 teaspoon vanilla extract
- 2 cups almond flour
- 1 teaspoon baking powder
- 1/2 teaspoon baking soda
- 1 teaspoon cinnamon
- 1/4 teaspoon salt
- Optional: 1/2 cup chopped walnuts or raisins

Directions:
1. Preheat the oven to 350°F (175°C). Grease a loaf pan.
2. Place shredded zucchini in a clean kitchen towel and squeeze out excess moisture.
3. In a large bowl, whisk together eggs, melted oil, honey/maple syrup, and vanilla extract.
4. Add almond flour, baking powder, baking soda, cinnamon, and salt to the wet ingredients. Mix until combined.
5. Fold in shredded zucchini and optional nuts or raisins.
6. Pour the batter into the prepared loaf pan.
7. Bake for 45-55 minutes or until a toothpick inserted into the center comes out clean.
8. Let the bread cool in the pan for 10 minutes before transferring to a wire rack to cool completely.

Recipe Variations:
- Incorporate grated carrots or apple for added moisture and flavor.
- Replace almond flour with a mix of almond and coconut flour for a different texture.

Topping Options:
- Serve slices with a dollop of Greek yogurt or a sprinkle of powdered sugar.

Customization Options:
- Make it dairy-free by using dairy-free yogurt in place of eggs.
- Adjust sweetness by adding more or less honey/maple syrup based on preference.

Important Notes:
- Ensure to squeeze excess moisture from the shredded zucchini to avoid a soggy loaf.
- Allow the bread to cool completely before slicing for better texture.

Nutritional Value: (Per slice - serves 10)
- Calories: ~220
- Total Fat: 15g
- Carbohydrates: 16g
- Fiber: 3g
- Protein: 6g

Pumpkin Bread

Preparation Time: 15 minutes **Cooking Time:** 50-60 minutes **Yield:** 1 loaf

Ingredients:
- 1 cup pumpkin puree
- 2 eggs
- 1/3 cup melted butter or coconut oil
- 1/2 cup honey or maple syrup
- 1 teaspoon vanilla extract
- 2 cups almond flour
- 1 teaspoon baking powder
- 1/2 teaspoon baking soda
- 1 teaspoon pumpkin pie spice
- 1/4 teaspoon salt
- Optional: 1/2 cup chopped pecans or cranberries

Directions:
1. Preheat the oven to 350°F (175°C). Grease a loaf pan.
2. In a large bowl, whisk together pumpkin puree, eggs, melted butter or oil, honey/maple syrup, and vanilla extract.
3. Add almond flour, baking powder, baking soda, pumpkin pie spice, and salt. Mix until well combined.
4. Fold in optional nuts or cranberries if desired.
5. Pour the batter into the prepared loaf pan.
6. Bake for 50-60 minutes or until a toothpick inserted into the center comes out clean.
7. Allow the bread to cool in the pan for 10 minutes before transferring to a wire rack to cool completely.

Recipe Variations:
- Incorporate a swirl of cream cheese into the batter for a delightful surprise.
- Replace some almond flour with oat flour for a slightly heartier texture.

Topping Options:
- Serve with a dollop of whipped cream or a sprinkle of cinnamon.

Customization Options:
- Make it gluten-free by ensuring all ingredients are gluten-free certified.
- Adjust sweetness by adding more or less honey/maple syrup based on preference.

Important Notes:
- Use canned pumpkin puree or homemade puree for best results.
- Let the bread cool completely before slicing for better texture.

Nutritional Value: (Per slice - serves 10)
- Calories: ~230
- Total Fat: 16g
- Carbohydrates: 18g
- Fiber: 3g
- Protein: 6g

Garlic Breadsticks

Preparation Time: 20 minutes **Cooking Time:** 15-20 minutes **Yield:** 12 breadsticks

Ingredients:
- 2 cups almond flour
- 1 teaspoon baking powder
- 1/2 teaspoon garlic powder
- 1/2 teaspoon dried oregano
- 1/4 teaspoon salt
- 2 large eggs
- 2 tablespoons olive oil
- 2 cloves garlic, minced
- 2 tablespoons chopped fresh parsley (optional)
- 2 tablespoons grated Parmesan cheese (optional)

Directions:
1. Preheat the oven to 350°F (175°C). Line a baking sheet with parchment paper.
2. In a bowl, mix almond flour, baking powder, garlic powder, oregano, and salt.
3. Add eggs and olive oil to the dry ingredients, mixing until a dough forms.
4. Divide the dough into 12 portions. Roll each portion into a stick shape and place on the prepared baking sheet.
5. In a small bowl, combine minced garlic and olive oil. Brush the breadsticks with this mixture.
6. Optional: Sprinkle chopped parsley and grated Parmesan cheese over the breadsticks.
7. Bake for 15-20 minutes or until golden brown.
8. Let the breadsticks cool slightly before serving.

Recipe Variations:
- Add shredded mozzarella or Italian seasoning to the dough for added flavor.
- Substitute garlic powder with fresh minced garlic for a stronger garlic taste.

Topping Options:
- Serve with marinara sauce or a garlic-infused olive oil for dipping.

Customization Options:
- Make them dairy-free by omitting the Parmesan cheese.
- Adjust the seasonings to suit personal preferences.

Important Notes:
- Keep an eye on the breadsticks while baking to prevent burning.
- These are best served fresh out of the oven for optimal taste and texture.

Nutritional Value: (Per breadstick - makes 12)
- Calories: ~100
- Total Fat: 9g
- Carbohydrates: 3g
- Fiber: 1g
- Protein: 4g

Flatbread/Naan

Preparation Time: 20 minutes (+ resting time) **Cooking Time:** 15-20 minutes **Yield:** 4-6 flatbreads/naans

Ingredients:
- 2 cups almond flour
- 2 tablespoons tapioca flour or arrowroot flour
- 1/2 teaspoon baking powder
- 1/4 teaspoon salt
- 1/2 cup Greek yogurt or dairy-free yogurt
- 1 egg, beaten
- 2 tablespoons olive oil

Directions:
1. In a bowl, combine almond flour, tapioca flour, baking powder, and salt.
2. Add Greek yogurt and beaten egg to the dry ingredients, mixing until a dough forms.
3. Divide the dough into 4-6 portions. Roll each portion into a ball.
4. On a floured surface, flatten each ball into a round flatbread/naan shape (about 1/4 inch thick).
5. Heat olive oil in a skillet over medium heat.
6. Cook each flatbread/naan for 2-3 minutes on each side or until golden brown spots appear.
7. Repeat the process with the remaining dough balls.
8. Serve warm.

Recipe Variations:
- Add minced garlic, chopped herbs, or spices like cumin or coriander to the dough for different flavors.
- Substitute part of the almond flour with coconut flour for a slightly different texture.

Topping Options:
- Brush with garlic butter or sprinkle with sesame seeds after cooking.

Customization Options:
- Make it vegan by using dairy-free yogurt and omitting the egg (adjust consistency as needed with additional liquid).
- Adjust the thickness of the flatbreads/naans based on preference.

Important Notes:
- Resting the dough for 10-15 minutes before rolling helps with easier handling.
- These can be stored in an airtight container for a day or two but are best fresh.

Nutritional Value: (Per flatbread/naan - makes 4)
- Calories: ~220
- Total Fat: 18g
- Carbohydrates: 8g
- Fiber: 4g
- Protein: 9g

Bagels

Preparation Time: 30 minutes (+ rising and baking time) **Cooking Time:** 20-25 minutes **Yield:** 4 bagels

Ingredients:
- 2 cups almond flour
- 1 tablespoon coconut flour
- 1 tablespoon baking powder
- 1/2 teaspoon garlic powder (optional)
- 1/2 teaspoon onion powder (optional)
- 1/4 teaspoon salt
- 2 large eggs
- 2 tablespoons melted butter or coconut oil
- 1 tablespoon honey or maple syrup
- Optional toppings: sesame seeds, poppy seeds, everything bagel seasoning

Directions:
1. Preheat the oven to 350°F (175°C). Line a baking sheet with parchment paper.
2. In a bowl, mix almond flour, coconut flour, baking powder, garlic powder, onion powder, and salt.
3. In another bowl, whisk eggs, melted butter or oil, and honey/maple syrup.
4. Combine the wet and dry ingredients until a dough forms.
5. Divide the dough into 4 portions. Roll each portion into a ball and then shape into a ring, creating a hole in the center.
6. Place the bagels on the prepared baking sheet.
7. Optional: Brush the tops of the bagels with beaten egg and sprinkle with desired toppings.
8. Bake for 20-25 minutes or until golden brown.
9. Allow the bagels to cool on a wire rack before slicing.

Recipe Variations:
- Add shredded cheese or herbs into the dough for different flavors.
- Incorporate seeds or nuts into the dough for added texture.

Topping Options:
- Serve with cream cheese, smoked salmon, or avocado.

Customization Options:
- Make them dairy-free by using coconut oil instead of butter.
- Adjust sweetness or omit honey/maple syrup based on preference.

Important Notes:
- Let the bagels cool completely before slicing for best texture.
- These can be toasted for a crispier texture.

Nutritional Value: (Per bagel - makes 4)
- Calories: ~330
- Total Fat: 28g
- Carbohydrates: 10g
- Fiber: 4g
- Protein: 12g

Lemon Bread

Preparation Time: 15 minutes **Cooking Time:** 45-50 minutes **Yield:** 1 loaf

Ingredients:
- 2 cups almond flour
- 1/4 cup coconut flour
- 1 teaspoon baking powder
- Zest of 2 lemons
- 1/3 cup lemon juice
- 1/2 cup honey or maple syrup
- 1/3 cup melted coconut oil or butter
- 4 eggs
- 1 teaspoon vanilla extract
- Optional: 1/4 cup poppy seeds or 1/2 cup blueberries

Directions:
1. Preheat the oven to 350°F (175°C). Grease a loaf pan.
2. In a bowl, mix almond flour, coconut flour, baking powder, and lemon zest.
3. In another bowl, whisk together lemon juice, honey/maple syrup, melted oil or butter, eggs, and vanilla extract.
4. Combine the wet and dry ingredients until well incorporated.
5. Fold in poppy seeds or blueberries if desired.
6. Pour the batter into the prepared loaf pan.
7. Bake for 45-50 minutes or until a toothpick inserted into the center comes out clean.
8. Let the bread cool in the pan for 10 minutes before transferring to a wire rack to cool completely.

Recipe Variations:
- Add a lemon glaze made with powdered sugar and lemon juice for extra sweetness.
- Replace some almond flour with cornmeal for a slightly different texture.

Topping Options:
- Dust with powdered sugar or drizzle with a lemon glaze.

Customization Options:
- Make it dairy-free by using coconut oil instead of butter.
- Adjust sweetness by adding more or less honey/maple syrup based on preference.

Important Notes:
- Ensure to use fresh lemon juice for the best flavor.
- Let the bread cool completely before slicing for better texture.

Nutritional Value: (Per slice - serves 10)
- Calories: ~240
- Total Fat: 18g
- Carbohydrates: 15g
- Fiber: 3g
- Protein: 7g

Blueberry Bread

Preparation Time: 15 minutes **Cooking Time:** 50-60 minutes **Yield:** 1 loaf

Ingredients:
- 2 cups almond flour
- 1/4 cup coconut flour
- 1 teaspoon baking powder
- 1/4 teaspoon salt
- 1/3 cup honey or maple syrup
- 1/4 cup melted coconut oil or butter
- 4 eggs
- 1 teaspoon vanilla extract
- 1 1/2 cups fresh or frozen blueberries

Directions:
1. Preheat the oven to 350°F (175°C). Grease a loaf pan.
2. In a bowl, whisk together almond flour, coconut flour, baking powder, and salt.
3. In another bowl, mix honey/maple syrup, melted oil or butter, eggs, and vanilla extract.
4. Combine the wet and dry ingredients until well combined.
5. Gently fold in the blueberries.
6. Pour the batter into the prepared loaf pan.
7. Bake for 50-60 minutes or until a toothpick inserted into the center comes out clean.
8. Let the bread cool in the pan for 10 minutes before transferring to a wire rack to cool completely.

Recipe Variations:
- Add lemon zest for a hint of citrusy flavor.
- Sprinkle a streusel topping made of almond flour, coconut oil, and a touch of sweetener for a crunchy top.

Topping Options:
- Serve with a dollop of whipped cream or a drizzle of honey.

Customization Options:
- Make it dairy-free by using coconut oil instead of butter.
- Adjust sweetness by adding more or less honey/maple syrup based on preference.

Important Notes:
- If using frozen blueberries, avoid thawing them before adding to the batter.
- Cool the bread completely before slicing for better texture.

Nutritional Value: (Per slice - serves 10)
- Calories: ~220
- Total Fat: 16g
- Carbohydrates: 15g
- Fiber: 3g
- Protein: 7g

Chocolate Bread

Preparation Time: 15 minutes **Cooking Time:** 50-60 minutes **Yield:** 1 loaf

Ingredients:
- 2 cups almond flour
- 1/4 cup coconut flour
- 1/3 cup unsweetened cocoa powder
- 1 teaspoon baking soda
- 1/4 teaspoon salt
- 1/3 cup honey or maple syrup
- 1/4 cup melted coconut oil or butter
- 4 eggs
- 1 teaspoon vanilla extract
- 1/2 cup dark chocolate chips (optional)

Directions:
1. Preheat the oven to 350°F (175°C). Grease a loaf pan.
2. In a bowl, whisk together almond flour, coconut flour, cocoa powder, baking soda, and salt.
3. In another bowl, mix honey/maple syrup, melted oil or butter, eggs, and vanilla extract.
4. Combine the wet and dry ingredients until well combined.
5. If using, fold in the dark chocolate chips.
6. Pour the batter into the prepared loaf pan.
7. Bake for 50-60 minutes or until a toothpick inserted into the center comes out clean.
8. Let the bread cool in the pan for 10 minutes before transferring to a wire rack to cool completely.

Recipe Variations:
- Add a tablespoon of instant coffee granules for a hint of mocha flavor.
- Sprinkle chopped nuts like walnuts or almonds for added texture.

Topping Options:
- Serve with a dusting of powdered sugar or a chocolate glaze.

Customization Options:
- Make it dairy-free by using dairy-free chocolate chips and coconut oil.
- Adjust sweetness by adding more or less honey/maple syrup based on preference.

Important Notes:
- Use high-quality cocoa powder for richer chocolate flavor.
- Cool the bread completely before slicing for better texture.

Nutritional Value: (Per slice - serves 10)
- Calories: ~230
- Total Fat: 17g
- Carbohydrates: 16g
- Fiber: 3g
- Protein: 7g

Apple Cinnamon Bread

Preparation Time: 15 minutes **Cooking Time:** 50-60 minutes **Yield:** 1 loaf

Ingredients:
- 2 cups almond flour
- 1/4 cup coconut flour
- 1 teaspoon baking powder
- 1/2 teaspoon baking soda
- 1 teaspoon ground cinnamon
- 1/4 teaspoon ground nutmeg
- 1/4 teaspoon salt
- 1/3 cup honey or maple syrup
- 1/4 cup melted coconut oil or butter
- 4 eggs
- 1 teaspoon vanilla extract
- 1 1/2 cups diced apples (peeled and cored)

Directions:
1. Preheat the oven to 350°F (175°C). Grease a loaf pan.
2. In a bowl, whisk together almond flour, coconut flour, baking powder, baking soda, cinnamon, nutmeg, and salt.
3. In another bowl, mix honey/maple syrup, melted oil or butter, eggs, and vanilla extract.
4. Combine the wet and dry ingredients until well combined.
5. Fold in the diced apples.
6. Pour the batter into the prepared loaf pan.
7. Bake for 50-60 minutes or until a toothpick inserted into the center comes out clean.
8. Let the bread cool in the pan for 10 minutes before transferring to a wire rack to cool completely.

Recipe Variations:
- Add a handful of raisins or chopped nuts for extra texture.

Topping Options:
- Serve with a dollop of Greek yogurt or a drizzle of honey.

Customization Options:
- Make it dairy-free by using coconut oil instead of butter.
- Adjust sweetness by adding more or less honey/maple syrup based on preference.

Important Notes:
- Use firm and tart apples for the best taste and texture.
- Cool the bread completely before slicing for better texture.

Nutritional Value: (Per slice - serves 10)
- Calories: ~220
- Total Fat: 16g
- Carbohydrates: 16g
- Fiber: 3g
- Protein: 7g

Cranberry Orange Bread

Preparation Time: 15 minutes **Cooking Time:** 50-60 minutes **Yield:** 1 loaf

Ingredients:
- 2 cups almond flour
- 1/4 cup coconut flour
- 1 teaspoon baking powder
- Zest of 1 orange
- 1/3 cup orange juice
- 1/3 cup honey or maple syrup
- 1/4 cup melted coconut oil or butter
- 4 eggs
- 1 teaspoon vanilla extract
- 1 cup fresh or frozen cranberries

Directions:
1. Preheat the oven to 350°F (175°C). Grease a loaf pan.
2. In a bowl, whisk together almond flour, coconut flour, baking powder, and orange zest.
3. In another bowl, mix orange juice, honey/maple syrup, melted oil or butter, eggs, and vanilla extract.
4. Combine the wet and dry ingredients until well combined.
5. Gently fold in the cranberries.
6. Pour the batter into the prepared loaf pan.
7. Bake for 50-60 minutes or until a toothpick inserted into the center comes out clean.
8. Let the bread cool in the pan for 10 minutes before transferring to a wire rack to cool completely.

Recipe Variations:
- Add a handful of chopped nuts like pecans or walnuts for added crunch.

Topping Options:
- Serve with a dusting of powdered sugar or a drizzle of orange glaze.

Customization Options:
- Make it dairy-free by using coconut oil instead of butter.
- Adjust sweetness by adding more or less honey/maple syrup based on preference.

Important Notes:
- If using frozen cranberries, avoid thawing them before adding to the batter.
- Cool the bread completely before slicing for better texture.

Nutritional Value: (Per slice - serves 10)
- Calories: ~220
- Total Fat: 16g
- Carbohydrates: 16g
- Fiber: 3g
- Protein: 7g

Carrot Bread

Preparation Time: 15 minutes **Cooking Time:** 50-60 minutes **Yield:** 1 loaf

Ingredients:
- 2 cups almond flour
- 1/4 cup coconut flour
- 1 teaspoon baking powder
- 1/2 teaspoon baking soda
- 1 teaspoon ground cinnamon
- 1/4 teaspoon ground nutmeg
- 1/4 teaspoon ground ginger
- 1/4 teaspoon salt
- 1/3 cup honey or maple syrup
- 1/4 cup melted coconut oil or butter
- 4 eggs
- 1 teaspoon vanilla extract
- 1 1/2 cups grated carrots

Directions:
1. Preheat the oven to 350°F (175°C). Grease a loaf pan.
2. In a bowl, whisk together almond flour, coconut flour, baking powder, baking soda, cinnamon, nutmeg, ginger, and salt.
3. In another bowl, mix honey/maple syrup, melted oil or butter, eggs, and vanilla extract.
4. Combine the wet and dry ingredients until well combined.
5. Fold in the grated carrots.
6. Pour the batter into the prepared loaf pan.
7. Bake for 50-60 minutes or until a toothpick inserted into the center comes out clean.
8. Let the bread cool in the pan for 10 minutes before transferring to a wire rack to cool completely.

Recipe Variations:
- Add shredded coconut or chopped nuts for additional texture.

Topping Options:
- Serve with a smear of cream cheese or a sprinkle of cinnamon.

Customization Options:
- Make it dairy-free by using coconut oil instead of butter.
- Adjust sweetness by adding more or less honey/maple syrup based on preference.

Important Notes:
- Use finely grated carrots for better incorporation into the batter.
- Cool the bread completely before slicing for better texture.

Nutritional Value: (Per slice - serves 10)
- Calories: ~220
- Total Fat: 16g
- Carbohydrates: 16g
- Fiber: 3g
- Protein: 7g

Cheddar Jalapeño Bread

Preparation Time: 15 minutes **Cooking Time:** 50-60 minutes **Yield:** 1 loaf

Ingredients:
- 2 cups almond flour
- 1/4 cup coconut flour
- 1 teaspoon baking powder
- 1/4 teaspoon salt
- 1/3 cup sour cream or Greek yogurt
- 1/4 cup melted butter or olive oil
- 4 eggs
- 1 cup shredded cheddar cheese
- 2-3 jalapeños, seeds removed and finely chopped

Directions:
1. Preheat the oven to 350°F (175°C). Grease a loaf pan.
2. In a bowl, whisk together almond flour, coconut flour, baking powder, and salt.
3. In another bowl, mix sour cream or Greek yogurt, melted butter or oil, and eggs until well combined.
4. Combine the wet and dry ingredients until a batter forms.
5. Gently fold in shredded cheddar cheese and chopped jalapeños.
6. Pour the batter into the prepared loaf pan.
7. Bake for 50-60 minutes or until a toothpick inserted into the center comes out clean.
8. Allow the bread to cool in the pan for 10 minutes before transferring to a wire rack to cool completely.

Recipe Variations:
- Add diced bacon for an extra flavor punch.
- Sprinkle some extra shredded cheddar on top before baking for a cheesy crust.

Topping Options:
- Serve with whipped cream cheese or a dollop of sour cream.

Customization Options:
- Adjust the spiciness by increasing or decreasing the amount of jalapeños used.

Important Notes:
- Ensure the jalapeños are finely chopped for even distribution in the bread.
- Cool completely before slicing for better texture.

Nutritional Value: (Per slice - serves 10)
- Calories: ~220
- Total Fat: 18g
- Carbohydrates: 6g
- Fiber: 3g
- Protein: 9g

Rosemary Olive Oil Bread

Preparation Time: 15 minutes **Cooking Time:** 50-60 minutes **Yield:** 1 loaf

Ingredients:
- 2 cups almond flour
- 1/4 cup coconut flour
- 1 teaspoon baking powder
- 1/2 teaspoon salt
- 1/4 cup extra virgin olive oil
- 4 eggs
- 1 tablespoon finely chopped fresh rosemary
- 1/4 cup chopped black or green olives

Directions:
1. Preheat the oven to 350°F (175°C). Grease a loaf pan.
2. In a bowl, whisk together almond flour, coconut flour, baking powder, and salt.
3. In another bowl, mix olive oil and eggs until well combined.
4. Combine the wet and dry ingredients until a batter forms.
5. Gently fold in chopped fresh rosemary and olives.
6. Pour the batter into the prepared loaf pan.
7. Bake for 50-60 minutes or until a toothpick inserted into the center comes out clean.
8. Let the bread cool in the pan for 10 minutes before transferring to a wire rack to cool completely.

Recipe Variations:
- Add sun-dried tomatoes for an extra burst of flavor.
- Brush the top of the bread with additional olive oil before baking for a shiny crust.

Topping Options:
- Serve with a drizzle of balsamic reduction or a side of olive tapenade.

Customization Options:
- Adjust the amount of rosemary or olives based on personal preference.

Important Notes:
- Fresh rosemary provides the best flavor for this bread.
- Cool completely before slicing for better texture.

Nutritional Value: (Per slice - serves 10)
- Calories: ~220
- Total Fat: 18g
- Carbohydrates: 6g
- Fiber: 3g
- Protein: 9g

Coconut Bread

Preparation Time: 15 minutes **Cooking Time:** 50-60 minutes **Yield:** 1 loaf

Ingredients:
- 2 cups almond flour
- 1/4 cup coconut flour
- 1 teaspoon baking powder
- 1/4 teaspoon salt
- 1/3 cup coconut milk
- 1/4 cup melted coconut oil
- 4 eggs
- 1/2 cup shredded unsweetened coconut

Directions:
1. Preheat the oven to 350°F (175°C). Grease a loaf pan.
2. In a bowl, whisk together almond flour, coconut flour, baking powder, and salt.
3. In another bowl, mix coconut milk, melted coconut oil, and eggs until well combined.
4. Combine the wet and dry ingredients until a batter forms.
5. Gently fold in shredded coconut.
6. Pour the batter into the prepared loaf pan.
7. Bake for 50-60 minutes or until a toothpick inserted into the center comes out clean.
8. Allow the bread to cool in the pan for 10 minutes before transferring to a wire rack to cool completely.

Recipe Variations:
- Add a teaspoon of coconut extract for an extra coconut flavor.
- Sprinkle additional shredded coconut on top before baking for added texture.

Topping Options:
- Serve slices with a smear of coconut butter or a sprinkle of powdered sugar.

Customization Options:
- Adjust sweetness by adding a touch of honey or maple syrup if desired.

Important Notes:
- Ensure to use unsweetened shredded coconut for a more natural flavor.
- Cool completely before slicing for better texture.

Nutritional Value: (Per slice - serves 10)
- Calories: ~220
- Total Fat: 18g
- Carbohydrates: 6g
- Fiber: 3g
- Protein: 9g

Raspberry Almond Bread

Preparation Time: 15 minutes **Cooking Time**: 50-60 minutes **Yield**: 1 loaf

Ingredients:
- 2 cups almond flour
- 1/4 cup coconut flour
- 1 teaspoon baking powder
- 1/4 teaspoon salt
- 1/3 cup honey or maple syrup
- 1/4 cup melted coconut oil or butter
- 4 eggs
- 1 teaspoon almond extract
- 1 cup fresh or frozen raspberries

Directions:
1. Preheat the oven to 350°F (175°C). Grease a loaf pan.
2. In a bowl, whisk together almond flour, coconut flour, baking powder, and salt.
3. In another bowl, mix honey/maple syrup, melted oil or butter, eggs, and almond extract until well combined.
4. Combine the wet and dry ingredients until a batter forms.
5. Gently fold in fresh or frozen raspberries.
6. Pour the batter into the prepared loaf pan.
7. Bake for 50-60 minutes or until a toothpick inserted into the center comes out clean.
8. Allow the bread to cool in the pan for 10 minutes before transferring to a wire rack to cool completely.

Recipe Variations:
- Add a handful of sliced almonds for a nutty crunch.
- Dust the top with powdered sugar after baking for a sweet finish.

Topping Options:
- Serve with a dollop of whipped cream or a sprinkle of sliced almonds.

Customization Options:
- Adjust sweetness by adding more or less honey/maple syrup based on preference.

Important Notes:
- If using frozen raspberries, avoid thawing them before adding to the batter.
- Cool completely before slicing for better texture.

Nutritional Value: (Per slice - serves 10)
- Calories: ~220
- Total Fat: 18g
- Carbohydrates: 6g
- Fiber: 3g
- Protein: 9g

Honey Almond Bread

Preparation Time: 15 minutes **Cooking Time:** 50-60 minutes **Yield:** 1 loaf

Ingredients:
- 2 cups almond flour
- 1/4 cup coconut flour
- 1 teaspoon baking powder
- 1/4 teaspoon salt
- 1/3 cup honey
- 1/4 cup melted coconut oil or butter
- 4 eggs
- 1 teaspoon almond extract
- 1/2 cup sliced almonds

Directions:
1. Preheat the oven to 350°F (175°C). Grease a loaf pan.
2. In a bowl, whisk together almond flour, coconut flour, baking powder, and salt.
3. In another bowl, mix honey, melted oil or butter, eggs, and almond extract until well combined.
4. Combine the wet and dry ingredients until a batter forms.
5. Gently fold in sliced almonds.
6. Pour the batter into the prepared loaf pan.
7. Bake for 50-60 minutes or until a toothpick inserted into the center comes out clean.
8. Allow the bread to cool in the pan for 10 minutes before transferring to a wire rack to cool completely.

Recipe Variations:
- Add a tablespoon of orange zest for a citrusy twist.
- Drizzle honey on top of the bread after baking for added sweetness.

Topping Options:
- Serve with a spread of honey butter or almond butter.

Customization Options:
- Adjust sweetness by adding more or less honey based on preference.

Important Notes:
- Cool completely before slicing for better texture.
- Toasting slices slightly before serving can enhance the flavor.

Nutritional Value: (Per slice - serves 10)
- Calories: ~220
- Total Fat: 18g
- Carbohydrates: 6g
- Fiber: 3g
- Protein: 9g

Spinach Feta Bread

Preparation Time: 15 minutes **Cooking Time:** 50-60 minutes **Yield:** 1 loaf

Ingredients:
- 2 cups almond flour
- 1/4 cup coconut flour
- 1 teaspoon baking powder
- 1/4 teaspoon salt
- 1/3 cup sour cream or Greek yogurt
- 1/4 cup melted butter or olive oil
- 4 eggs
- 1 cup chopped fresh spinach
- 1/2 cup crumbled feta cheese

Directions:
1. Preheat the oven to 350°F (175°C). Grease a loaf pan.
2. In a bowl, whisk together almond flour, coconut flour, baking powder, and salt.
3. In another bowl, mix sour cream or Greek yogurt, melted butter or oil, and eggs until well combined.
4. Combine the wet and dry ingredients until a batter forms.
5. Gently fold in chopped spinach and crumbled feta cheese.
6. Pour the batter into the prepared loaf pan.
7. Bake for 50-60 minutes or until a toothpick inserted into the center comes out clean.
8. Allow the bread to cool in the pan for 10 minutes before transferring to a wire rack to cool completely.

Recipe Variations:
- Add chopped sun-dried tomatoes for extra flavor.
- Top with a sprinkle of extra feta cheese before baking.

Topping Options:
- Serve with a side of tzatziki or hummus.

Customization Options:
- Adjust the amount of spinach or feta based on preference.

Important Notes:
- Cool completely before slicing for better texture.
- Serve warm or toasted for optimal taste.

Nutritional Value: (Per slice - serves 10)
- Calories: ~220
- Total Fat: 18g
- Carbohydrates: 6g
- Fiber: 3g
- Protein: 9g

Herb and Cheese Bread

Preparation Time: 15 minutes **Cooking Time:** 50-60 minutes **Yield:** 1 loaf

Ingredients:
- 2 cups almond flour
- 1/4 cup coconut flour
- 1 teaspoon baking powder
- 1/2 teaspoon salt
- 1/4 cup melted butter or olive oil
- 4 eggs
- 1 tablespoon chopped fresh herbs (such as parsley, basil, thyme)
- 1/2 cup shredded cheese (cheddar, mozzarella, or a blend)

Directions:
1. Preheat the oven to 350°F (175°C). Grease a loaf pan.
2. In a bowl, whisk together almond flour, coconut flour, baking powder, and salt.
3. In another bowl, mix melted butter or oil and eggs until well combined.
4. Combine the wet and dry ingredients until a batter forms.
5. Gently fold in chopped fresh herbs and shredded cheese.
6. Pour the batter into the prepared loaf pan.
7. Bake for 50-60 minutes or until a toothpick inserted into the center comes out clean.
8. Allow the bread to cool in the pan for 10 minutes before transferring to a wire rack to cool completely.

Recipe Variations:
- Add minced garlic for a garlic herb cheese bread.
- Sprinkle extra cheese on top before baking for a cheesy crust.

Topping Options:
- Serve with flavored butter or a side of marinara sauce.

Customization Options:
- Experiment with different herb combinations based on personal taste preferences.

Important Notes:
- Cool completely before slicing for better texture.
- Serve warm or toasted for enhanced flavors.

Nutritional Value: (Per slice - serves 10)
- Calories: ~220
- Total Fat: 18g
- Carbohydrates: 6g
- Fiber: 3g
- Protein: 9g

ALMOND FLOUR CRACKERS

Almond flour crackers are crispy and tasty, great with cheese or dips. They're a healthy snacking choice!

Almond Flour Crackers Recipe

Preparation Time: 10 minutes **Cooking Time:** 12-15 minutes

Ingredients:
- 2 cups almond flour
- 1 egg
- 2 tablespoons olive oil or melted butter
- 1/2 teaspoon salt (adjust to taste)
- 1/2 teaspoon garlic powder or any preferred herbs/spices (optional)
- Additional toppings or seeds (like sesame seeds, poppy seeds, flaxseeds) for added texture and flavor (optional)

Directions:
1. Preheat your oven to 350°F (175°C).
2. In a mixing bowl, combine the almond flour, egg, olive oil or melted butter, salt, and any additional spices/herbs if desired. Mix until it forms a dough.
3. Place the dough between two sheets of parchment paper and roll it out thinly. The thinner you roll the dough, the crispier the crackers will be.
4. Remove the top parchment paper and transfer the rolled-out dough (with the bottom parchment paper) onto a baking sheet.
5. Use a pizza cutter or a knife to cut the dough into small squares or rectangles to make the crackers.
6. Sprinkle any additional toppings or seeds on top and gently press them into the dough.
7. Bake in the preheated oven for 12-15 minutes or until the edges are golden brown and the crackers are crisp.
8. Allow the crackers to cool completely on a wire rack before breaking them apart along the scored lines.

Recipe Variations:

Herb and Garlic Crackers: Add garlic powder, dried herbs like rosemary, thyme, or oregano to the basic recipe for a savory twist.

Cheese Crackers: Mix in grated cheese (like cheddar, parmesan, or asiago) to the dough for a cheesy flavor.

Spicy Crackers: Incorporate cayenne pepper, paprika, or chili flakes for a kick of heat.

Everything Bagel Crackers: Sprinkle a mix of sesame seeds, poppy seeds, onion flakes, garlic flakes, and coarse salt on top of the dough before baking to mimic the flavors of an everything bagel.

Cracked Pepper Crackers: Add freshly cracked black pepper to the dough for a peppery taste.

Seed Crackers: Mix in various seeds like sesame seeds, pumpkin seeds, sunflower seeds, or flaxseeds into the dough for added texture and nutrition.

Sweet Cinnamon Crackers: Use almond flour, a sweetener like honey or maple syrup, and add cinnamon to the dough for a sweet, dessert-like cracker.

Rosemary Olive Oil Crackers: Combine almond flour with rosemary-infused olive oil for a fragrant and savory cracker.

Lemon Poppy Seed Crackers: Incorporate lemon zest and poppy seeds into the dough for a citrusy, crunchy snack.

Topping Options:
- Sesame seeds
- Poppy seeds
- Flaxseeds
- Coarse salt
- Herbs (rosemary, thyme, oregano)
- Cheese (grated cheddar, parmesan)

Customization Options:
Feel free to experiment with different seasonings, herbs, cheeses, and seeds to create various flavor combinations.

Important Notes:
Ensure the dough is rolled thinly for crispy crackers. Watch closely toward the end of baking to prevent burning, as almond flour can brown quickly.

Nutritional Value:
Nutritional values may vary based on added ingredients and toppings. On average, a serving of almond flour crackers (about 5-6 crackers) might contain approximately 150-180 calories, 12-15g of fat, 5-8g of protein, and 2-4g of carbohydrates, depending on the specific recipe and variations.

ALMOND FLOUR ENTREEES

Almond flour crusts make crunchy chicken or fish that's yummy and gluten-free. Goes well with veggies or salads.

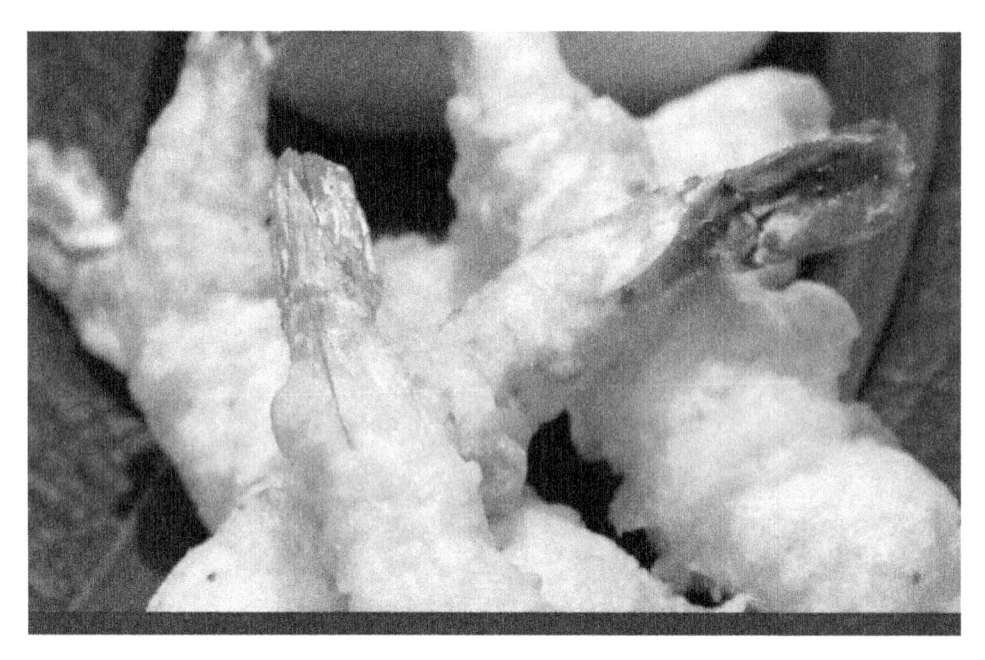

Almond Flour-Crusted Chicken

Preparation Time: 15 minutes **Cooking Time:** 20-25 minutes **Servings:** 4

Ingredients:
- 4 boneless, skinless chicken breasts
- 1 cup almond flour
- 1 tsp paprika
- 1 tsp garlic powder
- 1 tsp onion powder
- Salt and pepper to taste
- 2 eggs, beaten
- Olive oil or cooking spray

Directions:
1. Preheat the oven to 400°F (200°C).
2. In a shallow bowl, mix almond flour, paprika, garlic powder, onion powder, salt, and pepper.
3. Dip each chicken breast into the beaten eggs, then coat thoroughly with the almond flour mixture.
4. Place the coated chicken breasts on a baking sheet lined with parchment paper or greased with olive oil/cooking spray.
5. Bake for 20-25 minutes or until the chicken is cooked through and the coating is golden brown and crispy.
6. Serve hot with your preferred dipping sauce or alongside roasted vegetables.

Recipe Variations:
- Incorporate grated Parmesan cheese into the almond flour mixture for added flavor.
- Use different herbs or spices in the coating for a varied taste.

Topping Options:
- Serve with honey mustard, marinara sauce, or ranch dressing.

Customization Options:
- Adjust seasoning and spices in the almond flour coating to match personal taste preferences.

Important Notes:
- Ensure even coating of almond flour for a crispy texture.
- Opt for even-sized chicken breasts for uniform cooking.

Nutritional Value: (Per Serving)
- Calories: ~320
- Total Fat: 18g
- Carbohydrates: 4g
- Fiber: 2g
- Protein: 34g

Almond Flour-Coated Fish

Preparation Time: 15 minutes **Cooking Time:** 10-15 minutes **Servings:** 4

Ingredients:
- 4 fish fillets (cod, tilapia, salmon, etc.)
- 1 cup almond flour
- 1 tsp paprika
- 1 tsp garlic powder
- 1 tsp dried herbs (parsley, dill, etc.)
- Salt and pepper to taste
- 2 eggs, beaten
- Olive oil or cooking spray

Directions:
1. Preheat the oven to 400°F (200°C).
2. In a shallow bowl, mix almond flour, paprika, garlic powder, dried herbs, salt, and pepper.
3. Dip each fish fillet into the beaten eggs, then coat thoroughly with the almond flour mixture.
4. Place the coated fish fillets on a baking sheet lined with parchment paper or greased with olive oil/cooking spray.
5. Bake for 10-15 minutes, depending on the thickness of the fish, until it flakes easily with a fork and the coating is crispy and golden.
6. Serve hot with lemon wedges and a side salad or steamed vegetables.

Recipe Variations:
- Add grated lemon zest to the almond flour mixture for a zesty flavor.
- Experiment with different herbs or spices for diverse taste profiles.

Topping Options:
- Serve with tartar sauce, aioli, or a squeeze of fresh lemon.

Customization Options:
- Adjust the seasoning in the almond flour coating based on personal preferences.

Important Notes:
- Pat dry the fish fillets before coating for better adherence.
- Ensure even coating for consistent crisping while baking.

Nutritional Value: (Per Serving)
- Calories: ~250
- Total Fat: 15g
- Carbohydrates: 4g
- Fiber: 2g
- Protein: 26g

Almond Flour Pizza Crust

Preparation Time: 15 minutes **Cooking Time:** 20-25 minutes **Servings:** 4 (1 large pizza crust)

Ingredients:
- 2 cups almond flour
- 2 tbsp ground flaxseed meal
- 2 eggs
- 2 tbsp olive oil
- 1 tsp baking powder
- 1/2 tsp garlic powder
- 1/2 tsp dried oregano
- 1/2 tsp dried basil
- 1/2 tsp salt
- Pizza toppings of choice (sauce, cheese, vegetables, meats, etc.)

Directions:
1. Preheat the oven to 350°F (175°C). Line a baking sheet with parchment paper.
2. In a mixing bowl, combine almond flour, ground flaxseed meal, eggs, olive oil, baking powder, garlic powder, dried oregano, dried basil, and salt. Mix until a dough forms.
3. Place the dough onto the prepared baking sheet. Use your hands to press and shape the dough into a round or rectangular pizza crust, about 1/4-inch thick.
4. Bake the crust in the preheated oven for 15-18 minutes or until it starts to turn golden brown.
5. Remove the crust from the oven, add your desired pizza toppings, and return it to the oven for another 8-10 minutes or until the cheese is melted and bubbly.
6. Slice and serve hot.

Recipe Variations:
- Experiment with different herbs and spices in the crust for varied flavors.
- For a thinner crust, spread the dough thinner before baking.

Topping Options:
- Load with assorted vegetables, meats, and cheese for a customized pizza experience.

Customization Options:
- Adjust the seasoning in the crust to suit individual taste preferences.

Important Notes:
- Pre-bake the crust before adding toppings for a crispy base.
- Use a pizza stone for an even crispness on the crust.

Nutritional Value: (Per Serving - Crust Only)
- Calories: ~280
- Total Fat: 24g
- Carbohydrates: 8g
- Fiber: 4g
- Protein: 10g

Almond Flour Meatballs

Preparation Time: 15 minutes **Cooking Time:** 20-25 minutes **Servings:** Approximately 20 meatballs

Ingredients:
- 1 lb ground meat (beef, turkey, chicken, or a mix)
- 1 cup almond flour
- 2 eggs
- 1/4 cup grated Parmesan cheese
- 2 cloves garlic, minced
- 1 tsp dried oregano
- 1 tsp dried basil
- Salt and pepper to taste
- Olive oil for frying

Directions:
1. Preheat the oven to 375°F (190°C).
2. In a large mixing bowl, combine ground meat, almond flour, eggs, Parmesan cheese, minced garlic, dried oregano, dried basil, salt, and pepper. Mix until well combined.
3. Form the mixture into meatballs, about 1 to 1.5 inches in diameter.
4. Heat a skillet over medium heat with olive oil. Once hot, add the meatballs and cook for 2-3 minutes on each side until they are browned.
5. Transfer the browned meatballs to a baking dish and bake in the preheated oven for 15-20 minutes or until they are cooked through.
6. Serve hot with your favorite sauce or pasta.

Recipe Variations:
- Add chopped fresh parsley or other herbs for additional flavor.
- Use almond meal for a coarser texture in the meatballs.

Topping Options:
- Serve with marinara sauce, pesto, or as a topping for spaghetti.

Customization Options:
- Adjust seasoning and spices to match personal taste preferences.

Important Notes:
- Ensure even-sized meatballs for uniform cooking.
- Bake until internal temperature reaches 160°F (71°C) for safe consumption.

Nutritional Value: (Per Serving - 3 Meatballs)
- Calories: ~290
- Total Fat: 22g
- Carbohydrates: 4g
- Fiber: 2g
- Protein: 20g

Almond Flour-Coated Vegetables

Preparation Time: 15 minutes **Cooking Time:** 15-20 minutes **Servings:** 4

Ingredients:
- Assorted vegetables (zucchini, eggplant, cauliflower florets, bell peppers, etc.), sliced or cut into bite-sized pieces
- 1 cup almond flour
- 2 eggs, beaten
- Salt, pepper, and any preferred seasonings or herbs
- Olive oil or cooking spray

Directions:
1. Preheat the oven to 400°F (200°C). Line a baking sheet with parchment paper.
2. Prepare the vegetables by slicing or cutting them into similar-sized pieces.
3. In a shallow bowl, season almond flour with salt, pepper, and any other preferred seasonings.
4. Dip each piece of vegetable into the beaten eggs, then coat thoroughly with the almond flour mixture.
5. Place the coated vegetables on the prepared baking sheet in a single layer.
6. Drizzle or spray olive oil over the coated vegetables.
7. Bake for 15-20 minutes, turning halfway through, until the vegetables are tender and the coating is golden and crispy.
8. Serve hot as a side dish or a snack with your favorite dipping sauce.

Recipe Variations:
- Experiment with different spices or herbs to season the almond flour coating.
- Mix grated Parmesan cheese with almond flour for added flavor.

Topping Options:
- Pair with aioli, tzatziki, or a yogurt-based dip.

Customization Options:
- Customize seasoning according to personal flavor preferences.

Important Notes:
- Ensure vegetables are dry before coating for better adherence.
- Use a variety of colorful vegetables for a vibrant dish.

Nutritional Value: (Per Serving)
- Calories: ~220
- Total Fat: 16g
- Carbohydrates: 10g
- Fiber: 5g
- Protein: 8g

Almond Flour Quiche Crust

Preparation Time: 10 minutes **Cooking Time:** 15-20 minutes **Servings:** 1 crust (9-inch pie)

Ingredients:
- 1 1/2 cups almond flour
- 1/4 cup melted butter or olive oil
- 1/2 teaspoon salt
- 1 egg

Directions:
1. Preheat the oven to 350°F (175°C).
2. In a bowl, combine almond flour and salt.
3. Add the melted butter or olive oil and the egg to the almond flour mixture. Mix until a dough forms.
4. Press the dough evenly into a 9-inch pie dish to form the crust.
5. Use a fork to prick the crust in several places.
6. Bake the crust for 15-20 minutes until it's lightly golden.
7. Let it cool before adding your quiche filling.

Recipe Variations:
- Add herbs or spices (such as dried thyme or rosemary) to the crust mixture for added flavor.
- Substitute some of the almond flour with coconut flour for a different texture.

Topping Options:
- Fill with your favorite quiche ingredients like spinach, cheese, bacon, and onions.

Customization Options:
- Adjust the thickness of the crust to your preference by pressing it thinner or thicker in the pie dish.

Important Notes:
- Ensure the crust is fully cooked before adding quiche filling to prevent sogginess.

Nutritional Value: (Per Serving - Crust Only)
- Calories: ~180
- Total Fat: 16g
- Carbohydrates: 6g
- Fiber: 3g
- Protein: 6g

Almond Flour-Coated Pork Chops

Preparation Time: 15 minutes **Cooking Time:** 12-15 minutes **Servings:** 4 pork chops

Ingredients:
- 4 pork chops, bone-in or boneless
- 1 cup almond flour
- 1 teaspoon paprika
- 1 teaspoon garlic powder
- Salt and pepper to taste
- 2 eggs, beaten
- Olive oil or cooking spray

Directions:
1. Preheat the oven to 400°F (200°C).
2. In a shallow bowl, mix almond flour, paprika, garlic powder, salt, and pepper.
3. Dip each pork chop into the beaten eggs, then coat thoroughly with the almond flour mixture.
4. Place the coated pork chops on a baking sheet lined with parchment paper or greased with olive oil/cooking spray.
5. Bake for 12-15 minutes, turning halfway through, until the pork chops are cooked through and the coating is crispy.
6. Serve hot with a side of vegetables or mashed potatoes.

Recipe Variations:
- Add grated Parmesan cheese to the almond flour mixture for extra flavor.
- Incorporate dried herbs like thyme or sage into the coating for different taste profiles.

Topping Options:
- Pair with applesauce, gravy, or a tangy barbecue sauce.

Customization Options:
- Adjust seasoning and spices in the almond flour coating according to personal taste preferences.

Important Notes:
- Use a meat thermometer to ensure pork chops reach an internal temperature of 145°F (63°C) for safe consumption.

Nutritional Value: (Per Serving)
- Calories: ~300
- Total Fat: 18g
- Carbohydrates: 4g
- Fiber: 2g
- Protein: 30g

Almond Flour Chicken Tenders

Preparation Time: 15 minutes **Cooking Time:** 12-15 minutes **Servings:** 4

Ingredients:
- 1 lb chicken tenders or boneless, skinless chicken breasts, cut into strips
- 1 cup almond flour
- 1 teaspoon paprika
- 1 teaspoon garlic powder
- Salt and pepper to taste
- 2 eggs, beaten
- Olive oil or cooking spray

Directions:
1. Preheat the oven to 400°F (200°C).
2. In a shallow bowl, mix almond flour, paprika, garlic powder, salt, and pepper.
3. Dip each chicken tender into the beaten eggs, then coat thoroughly with the almond flour mixture.
4. Place the coated chicken tenders on a baking sheet lined with parchment paper or greased with olive oil/cooking spray.
5. Bake for 12-15 minutes, turning halfway through, until the chicken is cooked through and the coating is crispy.
6. Serve hot with your favorite dipping sauce or alongside a fresh salad.

Recipe Variations:
- Add a pinch of cayenne pepper for a spicy kick.
- Mix grated Parmesan cheese with almond flour for additional flavor.

Topping Options:
- Pair with honey mustard, ranch dressing, or a homemade aioli.

Customization Options:
- Adjust the seasoning in the almond flour coating based on personal preferences.

Important Notes:
- Ensure chicken tenders reach an internal temperature of 165°F (74°C) for safe consumption.

Nutritional Value: (Per Serving)
- Calories: ~280
- Total Fat: 18g
- Carbohydrates: 4g
- Fiber: 2g
- Protein: 26g

Almond Flour-Crusted Shrimp

Preparation Time: 15 minutes **Cooking Time:** 6-8 minutes **Servings:** 4

Ingredients:
- 1 lb large shrimp, peeled and deveined
- 1 cup almond flour
- 1 teaspoon paprika
- 1 teaspoon garlic powder
- Salt and pepper to taste
- 2 eggs, beaten
- Olive oil or cooking spray

Directions:
1. Preheat the oven to 400°F (200°C).
2. In a shallow bowl, mix almond flour, paprika, garlic powder, salt, and pepper.
3. Dip each shrimp into the beaten eggs, then coat thoroughly with the almond flour mixture.
4. Place the coated shrimp on a baking sheet lined with parchment paper or greased with olive oil/cooking spray.
5. Bake for 6-8 minutes until the shrimp are pink and the coating is crispy.
6. Serve hot with a squeeze of fresh lemon and your favorite dipping sauce.

Recipe Variations:
- Add a pinch of cayenne pepper or chili flakes for a spicy version.
- Incorporate grated coconut into the almond flour mixture for a tropical twist.

Topping Options:
- Pair with cocktail sauce, tartar sauce, or a mango salsa.

Customization Options:
- Adjust seasoning and spices in the almond flour coating to suit taste preferences.

Important Notes:
- Keep an eye on shrimp to prevent overcooking as they cook quickly.

Nutritional Value: (Per Serving)
- Calories: ~240
- Total Fat: 14g
- Carbohydrates: 4g
- Fiber: 2g
- Protein: 24g

Almond Flour Onion Rings

Preparation Time: 15 minutes **Cooking Time:** 15-20 minutes **Servings:** 4

Ingredients:
- 2 large onions, cut into rings
- 1 cup almond flour
- 1 teaspoon paprika
- 1 teaspoon garlic powder
- Salt and pepper to taste
- 2 eggs, beaten
- Olive oil or cooking spray

Directions:
1. Preheat the oven to 400°F (200°C).
2. In a shallow bowl, mix almond flour, paprika, garlic powder, salt, and pepper.
3. Dip each onion ring into the beaten eggs, then coat thoroughly with the almond flour mixture.
4. Place the coated onion rings on a baking sheet lined with parchment paper or greased with olive oil/cooking spray.
5. Bake for 15-20 minutes until the onion rings are crispy and golden brown.
6. Serve hot as a side dish or a crunchy snack.

Recipe Variations:
- Incorporate grated Parmesan cheese into the almond flour mixture for extra flavor.
- Add a pinch of cayenne pepper for a spicy kick.

Topping Options:
- Dip in ketchup, barbecue sauce, or a creamy garlic aioli.

Customization Options:
- Adjust seasoning and spices to match personal preferences.

Important Notes:
- Ensure even coating for uniform crisping.

Nutritional Value: (Per Serving)
- Calories: ~180
- Total Fat: 12g
- Carbohydrates: 12g
- Fiber: 4g
- Protein: 8g

Almond Flour Crispy Tofu

Preparation Time: 30 minutes **Cooking Time:** 25 minutes **Servings:** 4

Ingredients:
- 1 block (14 oz) firm tofu, drained and pressed
- 1 cup almond flour
- 1 teaspoon garlic powder
- 1 teaspoon paprika
- Salt and pepper to taste
- 2 eggs, beaten
- Olive oil or cooking spray

Directions:
1. Preheat the oven to 400°F (200°C).
2. Cut the tofu into cubes or strips.
3. In a shallow bowl, mix almond flour, garlic powder, paprika, salt, and pepper.
4. Dip each piece of tofu into the beaten eggs, then coat thoroughly with the almond flour mixture.
5. Place the coated tofu on a baking sheet lined with parchment paper or greased with olive oil/cooking spray.
6. Bake for 20-25 minutes, turning halfway through, until the tofu is crispy and golden.
7. Serve hot with your preferred dipping sauce or alongside a fresh salad.

Recipe Variations:
- Add sesame seeds or grated coconut to the almond flour mixture for added texture.
- Incorporate a dash of soy sauce or Sriracha into the egg wash for extra flavor.

Topping Options:
- Pair with a sweet chili sauce, teriyaki glaze, or peanut dipping sauce.

Customization Options:
- Adjust seasoning and spices in the almond flour coating based on personal taste preferences.

Important Notes:
- Use extra firm tofu for better texture.
- Flip the tofu gently to prevent the coating from coming off.

Nutritional Value: (Per Serving)
- Calories: ~240
- Total Fat: 16g
- Carbohydrates: 8g
- Fiber: 4g
- Protein: 18g

Almond Flour Breaded Eggplant

Preparation Time: 20 minutes **Cooking Time:** 20-25 minutes **Servings:** 4

Ingredients:
- 1 large eggplant, sliced into rounds
- 1 cup almond flour
- 1 teaspoon Italian seasoning
- 1/2 teaspoon garlic powder
- Salt and pepper to taste
- 2 eggs, beaten
- Olive oil or cooking spray

Directions:
1. Preheat the oven to 400°F (200°C). Line a baking sheet with parchment paper.
2. In a shallow bowl, mix almond flour, Italian seasoning, garlic powder, salt, and pepper.
3. Dip each eggplant slice into the beaten eggs, then coat thoroughly with the almond flour mixture.
4. Place the coated eggplant slices on the prepared baking sheet.
5. Drizzle or spray olive oil over the coated eggplant slices.
6. Bake for 20-25 minutes until the eggplant is tender and the coating is crispy.
7. Serve hot as a side dish or layer in a sandwich.

Recipe Variations:
- Incorporate grated Parmesan cheese into the almond flour mixture for added flavor.
- Use different herbs like basil or oregano for diverse taste profiles.

Topping Options:
- Pair with marinara sauce for eggplant parmesan or serve with a garlic aioli.

Customization Options:
- Adjust seasoning and spices in the almond flour coating according to personal preferences.

Important Notes:
- Salt the eggplant slices and let them sit for 10-15 minutes to draw out excess moisture before coating.

Nutritional Value: (Per Serving)
- Calories: ~180
- Total Fat: 12g
- Carbohydrates: 14g
- Fiber: 8g
- Protein: 10g

Almond Flour-Coated Cauliflower

Preparation Time: 20 minutes **Cooking Time:** 25-30 minutes **Servings:** 4

Ingredients:
- 1 head cauliflower, cut into florets
- 1 cup almond flour
- 1 teaspoon smoked paprika
- 1 teaspoon onion powder
- Salt and pepper to taste
- 2 eggs, beaten
- Olive oil or cooking spray

Directions:
1. Preheat the oven to 400°F (200°C). Line a baking sheet with parchment paper.
2. In a shallow bowl, mix almond flour, smoked paprika, onion powder, salt, and pepper.
3. Dip each cauliflower floret into the beaten eggs, then coat thoroughly with the almond flour mixture.
4. Place the coated cauliflower florets on the prepared baking sheet.
5. Drizzle or spray olive oil over the coated cauliflower florets.
6. Bake for 25-30 minutes, turning halfway through, until the cauliflower is tender and the coating is crispy.
7. Serve hot as a side dish or a delicious snack.

Recipe Variations:
- Add a pinch of cayenne pepper for a spicy kick.
- Mix in grated Parmesan cheese for added flavor.

Topping Options:
- Pair with a creamy ranch dressing, buffalo sauce, or a tahini dip.

Customization Options:
- Adjust seasoning and spices in the almond flour coating according to personal taste preferences.

Important Notes:
- Ensure cauliflower florets are dry before coating to help the almond flour stick better.

Nutritional Value: (Per Serving)
- Calories: ~150
- Total Fat: 10g
- Carbohydrates: 10g
- Fiber: 6g
- Protein: 8g

Almond Flour Turkey Burgers

Preparation Time: 15 minutes **Cooking Time:** 12-15 minutes **Servings:** 4

Ingredients:
- 1 lb ground turkey
- 1/2 cup almond flour
- 1 teaspoon garlic powder
- 1 teaspoon onion powder
- 1 teaspoon smoked paprika
- Salt and pepper to taste
- Olive oil for cooking
- Hamburger buns and desired toppings

Directions:
1. In a mixing bowl, combine ground turkey, almond flour, garlic powder, onion powder, smoked paprika, salt, and pepper. Mix until well combined.
2. Divide the mixture into 4 equal portions and shape them into burger patties.
3. Heat olive oil in a skillet over medium heat.
4. Cook the turkey burgers for 5-7 minutes on each side until they are cooked through and reach an internal temperature of 165°F (74°C).
5. Serve the burgers on buns with your favorite toppings.

Recipe Variations:
- Add grated cheese or chopped herbs into the turkey mixture for added flavor.
- Experiment with different spices or seasonings according to preference.

Topping Options:
- Top with lettuce, tomato, onions, pickles, cheese, avocado, or your preferred burger toppings.

Customization Options:
- Customize the seasoning in the turkey burger mixture based on taste preferences.

Important Notes:
- Use lean ground turkey for healthier burgers.
- Avoid pressing down on the burgers while cooking to retain juices.

Nutritional Value: (Per Serving - Patty Only)
- Calories: ~200
- Total Fat: 10g
- Carbohydrates: 2g
- Fiber: 1g
- Protein: 25g

Almond Flour-Coated Cheese Sticks

Preparation Time: 20 minutes **Cooking Time:** 6-8 minutes **Servings:** 4

Ingredients:
- 8 mozzarella cheese sticks
- 1 cup almond flour
- 1 teaspoon Italian seasoning
- 1/2 teaspoon garlic powder
- Salt and pepper to taste
- 2 eggs, beaten
- Olive oil or cooking spray

Directions:
1. Preheat the oven to 400°F (200°C). Line a baking sheet with parchment paper.
2. In a shallow bowl, mix almond flour, Italian seasoning, garlic powder, salt, and pepper.
3. Dip each mozzarella stick into the beaten eggs, then coat thoroughly with the almond flour mixture.
4. Place the coated cheese sticks on the prepared baking sheet.
5. Freeze the coated cheese sticks for 15-20 minutes to firm up.
6. Bake for 6-8 minutes until the cheese is melty and the coating is crispy.
7. Serve hot with marinara sauce or your favorite dipping sauce.

Recipe Variations:
- Add a pinch of cayenne pepper or chili flakes for a spicy version.
- Mix grated Parmesan cheese with almond flour for additional flavor.

Topping Options:
- Pair with marinara sauce, salsa, or a chipotle mayo dip.

Customization Options:
- Adjust seasoning and spices in the almond flour coating to suit taste preferences.

Important Notes:
- Freezing the cheese sticks before baking helps them hold their shape and prevents excessive melting.

Nutritional Value: (Per Serving - 2 Cheese Sticks)
- Calories: ~280
- Total Fat: 20g
- Carbohydrates: 6g
- Fiber: 2g
- Protein: 18g

Almond Flour-Coated Mushroom Caps

Preparation Time: 20 minutes **Cooking Time:** 15-20 minutes **Servings:** 4

Ingredients:
- 12-16 large mushroom caps, cleaned and stems removed
- 1 cup almond flour
- 1 teaspoon dried thyme
- 1/2 teaspoon onion powder
- Salt and pepper to taste
- 2 eggs, beaten
- Olive oil or cooking spray

Directions:
1. Preheat the oven to 375°F (190°C). Line a baking sheet with parchment paper.
2. In a shallow bowl, mix almond flour, dried thyme, onion powder, salt, and pepper.
3. Dip each mushroom cap into the beaten eggs, then coat thoroughly with the almond flour mixture.
4. Place the coated mushroom caps on the prepared baking sheet.
5. Drizzle or spray olive oil over the coated mushroom caps.
6. Bake for 15-20 minutes until the mushrooms are tender and the coating is crispy.
7. Serve hot as an appetizer or a side dish.

Recipe Variations:
- Add grated Parmesan cheese into the almond flour mixture for extra flavor.
- Use different herbs like rosemary or basil for varied taste profiles.

Topping Options:
- Serve with a balsamic glaze, garlic aioli, or a creamy herb dip.

Customization Options:
- Adjust seasoning and spices in the almond flour coating based on personal preferences.

Important Notes:
- Remove excess moisture from mushroom caps to help the almond flour coating adhere better.

Nutritional Value: (Per Serving - 4 Mushroom Caps)
- Calories: ~150
- Total Fat: 10g
- Carbohydrates: 8g
- Fiber: 4g
- Protein: 8g

ALMOND FLOUR PIE RECIPES

Almond flour pie crusts are flaky and add a nutty taste to pies. Perfect for fruity or creamy fillings.

Almond Flour Apple Pie

Preparation Time: 30 minutes **Cooking Time:** 45-50 minutes **Servings:** 8 slices

Ingredients:
- 2 1/2 cups almond flour
- 1/2 cup unsalted butter, cold and cubed
- 1/4 cup cold water
- 6 cups peeled and sliced apples (mix of Granny Smith and Honeycrisp)
- 1/2 cup granulated sugar
- 2 tablespoons lemon juice
- 1 teaspoon ground cinnamon
- 1/4 teaspoon nutmeg
- 1 tablespoon cornstarch or arrowroot powder
- 1 egg (for egg wash)
- Optional: Additional sugar for sprinkling on top

Directions:
1. Preheat the oven to 375°F (190°C).
2. In a bowl, combine almond flour and cold, cubed butter. Use a pastry cutter or fork to mix until it resembles coarse crumbs.
3. Slowly add cold water, one tablespoon at a time, until the dough comes together.
4. Form the dough into a ball, wrap it in plastic wrap, and refrigerate for 15-20 minutes.
5. In a large bowl, toss sliced apples with sugar, lemon juice, cinnamon, nutmeg, and cornstarch.
6. Roll out two-thirds of the almond flour dough on a lightly floured surface to fit a pie dish. Place the rolled dough in the pie dish.
7. Add the apple filling into the pie crust.
8. Roll out the remaining dough to cover the pie or create a lattice crust.
9. Beat the egg and brush it over the pie crust. Sprinkle sugar on top if desired.
10. Bake for 45-50 minutes or until the crust is golden brown and the filling is bubbling.
11. Allow the pie to cool before slicing.

Recipe Variations:
- Mix in other fruits like cranberries or raisins for added flavor and texture.
- Experiment with different spices such as cloves or ginger in the apple filling.

Topping Options:
- Serve with vanilla ice cream, whipped cream, or a dollop of Greek yogurt.

Customization Options:
- Adjust sugar and spice levels in the filling to suit personal taste preferences.

Important Notes:
- Allow the pie to cool adequately before slicing to set the filling.
- Cover the pie edges with foil if they brown too quickly while baking.

Nutritional Value: (Per Serving)
- Calories: ~350
- Total Fat: 26g
- Carbohydrates: 28g
- Fiber: 7g
- Protein: 7g

Almond Flour Pumpkin Pie

Preparation Time: 30 minutes **Cooking Time:** 50-55 minutes **Servings:** 8 slices

Ingredients:
- 1 1/2 cups almond flour
- 1/4 cup unsalted butter, melted
- 1 can (15 oz) pumpkin puree
- 3/4 cup full-fat coconut milk or heavy cream
- 2 eggs
- 1/2 cup brown sugar or coconut sugar
- 1 teaspoon vanilla extract
- 1 teaspoon ground cinnamon
- 1/2 teaspoon ground ginger
- 1/4 teaspoon ground cloves
- 1/4 teaspoon nutmeg
- 1/4 teaspoon salt

Directions:
1. Preheat the oven to 350°F (175°C).
2. In a bowl, mix almond flour and melted butter until combined. Press the mixture into a pie dish to form the crust.
3. In another bowl, whisk together pumpkin puree, coconut milk (or heavy cream), eggs, sugar, vanilla extract, spices, and salt until smooth.
4. Pour the pumpkin mixture into the prepared almond flour crust.
5. Bake for 50-55 minutes or until the center of the pie is set.
6. Allow the pie to cool completely before slicing.

Recipe Variations:
- Add a tablespoon of bourbon for an extra depth of flavor.
- Use a graham cracker crust made with almond flour for a different crust variation.

Topping Options:
- Serve with whipped cream, a sprinkle of cinnamon, or a drizzle of maple syrup.

Customization Options:
- Adjust sweetness by altering the amount of sugar used.
- Experiment with different spices for varied flavor profiles.

Important Notes:
- Use pure pumpkin puree, not pumpkin pie filling, for this recipe.
- Let the pie cool thoroughly to set before slicing.

Nutritional Value: (Per Serving)
- Calories: ~260
- Total Fat: 20g
- Carbohydrates: 16g
- Fiber: 4g
- Protein: 6g

Almond Flour Pecan Pie

Preparation Time: 20 minutes **Cooking Time:** 50-55 minutes **Servings:** 8 slices

Ingredients:
- 2 1/2 cups almond flour
- 1/2 cup unsalted butter, melted
- 1 cup packed brown sugar or coconut sugar
- 3/4 cup corn syrup or maple syrup
- 3 eggs
- 1 teaspoon vanilla extract
- 1/4 teaspoon salt
- 1 1/2 cups pecan halves

Directions:
1. Preheat the oven to 350°F (175°C).
2. In a bowl, combine almond flour and melted butter. Press the mixture into a pie dish to form the crust.
3. In another bowl, whisk together brown sugar, corn syrup (or maple syrup), eggs, vanilla extract, and salt until well combined.
4. Stir in the pecan halves.
5. Pour the pecan mixture into the prepared almond flour crust.
6. Bake for 50-55 minutes or until the center of the pie is set.
7. Allow the pie to cool completely before serving.

Recipe Variations:
- Add a sprinkle of sea salt on top before baking for a salted caramel flavor.
- Use a mix of different nuts like walnuts or almonds with pecans.

Topping Options:
- Serve with a scoop of vanilla ice cream or a dollop of whipped cream.

Customization Options:
- Adjust sweetness by altering the amount of sugar or syrup used.
- Toast the pecans before adding them for enhanced flavor.

Important Notes:
- Be cautious not to overmix the pecan pie filling.
- Let the pie cool entirely before slicing.

Nutritional Value: (Per Serving)
- Calories: ~380
- Total Fat: 28g
- Carbohydrates: 30g
- Fiber: 4g
- Protein: 7g

Almond Flour Berry Pie

Preparation Time: 30 minutes **Cooking Time:** 45-50 minutes

Ingredients:
- 2 1/2 cups almond flour
- 1/2 cup unsalted butter, cold and cubed
- 1/4 cup cold water
- 4 cups mixed berries (strawberries, blueberries, raspberries)
- 1/2 cup granulated sugar or sweetener of choice
- 2 tablespoons cornstarch or arrowroot powder
- Zest and juice of 1 lemon
- 1 egg (for egg wash)
- Optional: Additional sugar for sprinkling on top

Directions:
1. Preheat the oven to 375°F (190°C).
2. In a bowl, combine almond flour and cold, cubed butter. Use a pastry cutter or fork to mix until it resembles coarse crumbs.
3. Slowly add cold water, one tablespoon at a time, until the dough comes together.
4. Form the dough into a ball, wrap it in plastic wrap, and refrigerate for 15-20 minutes.
5. In a large bowl, toss mixed berries with sugar, cornstarch, lemon zest, and lemon juice.
6. Roll out two-thirds of the almond flour dough on a lightly floured surface to fit a pie dish. Place the rolled dough in the pie dish.
7. Add the berry filling into the pie crust.
8. Roll out the remaining dough to cover the pie or create a lattice crust.
9. Beat the egg and brush it over the pie crust. Sprinkle sugar on top if desired.
10. Bake for 45-50 minutes or until the crust is golden brown and the filling is bubbling.
11. Allow the pie to cool before slicing.

Recipe Variations:
- Use a single type of berry or a combination based on preference and availability.
- Add a touch of almond extract to complement the almond flour crust.

Topping Options:
- Serve with a scoop of vanilla ice cream or a dollop of whipped cream.

Customization Options:
- Adjust sugar levels in the filling based on the sweetness of the berries.

Important Notes:
- Let the pie cool adequately to set the filling and avoid a runny pie.

Nutritional Value: (Per Serving)
- Calories: ~320
- Total Fat: 22g
- Carbohydrates: 28g
- Fiber: 7g
- Protein: 6g

Almond Flour Chocolate Pie

Preparation Time: 30 minutes **Cooking Time:** 45-50 minutes **Servings:** 8 slices

Ingredients:
- 2 1/2 cups almond flour
- 1/2 cup unsalted butter, cold and cubed
- 1/4 cup cold water
- 1 cup dark chocolate chips or chopped dark chocolate
- 1 cup full-fat coconut milk or heavy cream
- 1/2 cup granulated sugar or sweetener of choice
- 3 eggs
- 1 teaspoon vanilla extract
- Pinch of salt

Directions:

1. Preheat the oven to 375°F (190°C).
2. In a bowl, combine almond flour and cold, cubed butter. Use a pastry cutter or fork to mix until it resembles coarse crumbs.
3. Slowly add cold water, one tablespoon at a time, until the dough comes together.
4. Form the dough into a ball, wrap it in plastic wrap, and refrigerate for 15-20 minutes.
5. In a saucepan, heat the coconut milk (or heavy cream) until it starts to simmer. Remove from heat and add the chocolate chips. Let it sit for a few minutes, then stir until smooth.
6. In a separate bowl, whisk together sugar, eggs, vanilla extract, and a pinch of salt.
7. Slowly pour the chocolate mixture into the egg mixture, whisking continuously until well combined.
8. Roll out two-thirds of the almond flour dough on a lightly floured surface to fit a pie dish. Place the rolled dough in the pie dish.
9. Pour the chocolate filling into the pie crust.
10. Roll out the remaining dough to cover the pie or create a lattice crust.
11. Bake for 45-50 minutes or until the crust is golden brown and the filling is set.
12. Allow the pie to cool before slicing.

Recipe Variations:
- Use milk or white chocolate for a different flavor profile.
- Incorporate a tablespoon of instant espresso for a mocha twist.

Topping Options:
- Serve with a dollop of whipped cream or a scoop of vanilla ice cream.

Customization Options:
- Adjust sweetness by altering the amount of sugar used.

Important Notes:
- Allow the pie to cool thoroughly before slicing to set the filling.
- Cover the pie edges with foil if they brown too quickly while baking.

Nutritional Value: (Per Serving)
- Calories: ~380
- Total Fat: 30g
- Carbohydrates: 26g
- Fiber: 5g
- Protein: 8g

ALMOND FLOUR PASTRIES

Enjoy buttery almond flour pastries, like croissants or Danish pastries. They're gluten-free and go well with coffee or tea.

Almond Flour Croissants

Preparation Time: 1 hour + 8-12 hours (chilling time) **Cooking Time:** 15-20 minutes **Servings:** 8 croissants

Ingredients:
- 2 cups almond flour
- 1/4 cup coconut flour
- 1/4 cup cold butter, cubed
- 2 tablespoons erythritol or sweetener of choice
- 1/2 teaspoon salt
- 2 large eggs, divided
- 1 teaspoon baking powder
- 8 ounces cream cheese, softened
- 1 teaspoon vanilla extract
- 1 tablespoon almond milk
- Sliced almonds for topping (optional)

Directions:
1. In a food processor, pulse almond flour, coconut flour, cold butter cubes, sweetener, salt, 1 egg, and baking powder until a dough forms.
2. Wrap the dough in plastic wrap and refrigerate for 8-12 hours or overnight.
3. Preheat the oven to 375°F (190°C) and line a baking sheet with parchment paper.
4. In a bowl, mix cream cheese, vanilla extract, almond milk, and the remaining egg until smooth.
5. Roll out the chilled dough on a lightly floured surface into a rectangle, then cut into triangles.
6. Spread a small amount of the cream cheese mixture on each triangle and roll them into croissant shapes.
7. Place the croissants on the prepared baking sheet, brush the tops with beaten egg, and sprinkle sliced almonds if desired.
8. Bake for 15-20 minutes until golden brown.
9. Let them cool slightly before serving.

Recipe Variations:
- Add a layer of sugar-free jam or chocolate spread before rolling for flavored croissants.
- Sprinkle cinnamon and erythritol for a sweet twist.

Topping Options:
- Dust with powdered erythritol or drizzle with sugar-free glaze for added sweetness.

Customization Options:
- Experiment with different fillings or toppings to create varied flavors.

Important Notes:
- Ensure the dough is adequately chilled for best results in achieving flakiness.

Nutritional Value: (Per Croissant)
- Calories: ~290
- Total Fat: 25g
- Carbohydrates: 7g
- Fiber: 3g
- Protein: 9g

Almond Flour Danish Pastries

Preparation Time: 1 hour + 8-12 hours (chilling time) **Cooking Time:** 15-20 minutes **Servings:** 8 pastries

Ingredients:
- 2 cups almond flour
- 1/4 cup coconut flour
- 1/4 cup cold butter, cubed
- 2 tablespoons erythritol or sweetener of choice
- 1/2 teaspoon salt
- 2 large eggs, divided
- 1 teaspoon baking powder
- 8 ounces cream cheese, softened
- 1 teaspoon vanilla extract
- 1 tablespoon almond milk
- Sugar-free fruit preserves or pie filling for topping

Directions:
1. Follow steps 1-3 from the Almond Flour Croissants recipe to prepare the dough and refrigerate it.
2. In a bowl, mix cream cheese, vanilla extract, almond milk, and one egg until smooth.
3. Roll out the chilled dough on a lightly floured surface into a rectangle.
4. Cut the rectangle into squares and make a diagonal cut from each corner, leaving the center uncut.
5. Spoon a small amount of cream cheese mixture into the center of each square and top with a teaspoon of fruit preserves or pie filling.
6. Fold alternate corners of each square into the center, slightly overlapping, to create a Danish pastry shape.
7. Place the pastries on a lined baking sheet, brush with beaten egg, and bake for 15-20 minutes until golden brown.
8. Let them cool before serving.

Recipe Variations:
- Use different flavored fillings like lemon curd, blueberry, raspberry, or apple pie filling.
- Sprinkle sliced almonds or powdered erythritol on top before baking for added texture and sweetness.

Topping Options:
- Drizzle with a sugar-free glaze or sprinkle with powdered erythritol after baking.

Customization Options:
- Experiment with various fruit fillings or combine different flavors for variety.

Important Notes:
- Properly chill the dough for the best texture and flakiness.

Nutritional Value: (Per Pastry)
- Calories: ~280
- Total Fat: 24g
- Carbohydrates: 7g
- Fiber: 3g
- Protein: 8g

Almond Flour Scones

Preparation Time: 20 minutes **Cooking Time:** 15-18 minutes **Servings:** 8 scones

Ingredients:
- 2 cups almond flour
- 1/4 cup coconut flour
- 1/4 cup erythritol or sweetener of choice
- 1 teaspoon baking powder
- 1/4 teaspoon salt
- 1/4 cup cold butter, cubed
- 1/4 cup heavy cream or coconut cream
- 1 large egg
- 1 teaspoon vanilla extract
- 1/2 cup fresh berries or sugar-free chocolate chips (optional)

Directions:
1. Preheat the oven to 350°F (175°C) and line a baking sheet with parchment paper.
2. In a mixing bowl, combine almond flour, coconut flour, erythritol, baking powder, and salt.
3. Cut in the cold butter cubes using a pastry cutter or fork until the mixture resembles coarse crumbs.
4. In a separate bowl, whisk together heavy cream, egg, and vanilla extract.
5. Pour the wet ingredients into the dry ingredients and stir until a dough forms.
6. Gently fold in fresh berries or sugar-free chocolate chips if using.
7. Form the dough into a ball and place it on the prepared baking sheet.
8. Flatten the dough into a circle about 1-inch thick, then cut it into 8 wedges.
9. Bake for 15-18 minutes until the scones are golden brown.
10. Allow them to cool slightly before serving.

Recipe Variations:
- Add lemon zest or almond extract for different flavor profiles.
- Mix in chopped nuts or dried fruits for added texture.

Topping Options:
- Serve with sugar-free jam, clotted cream, or a dollop of whipped cream.

Customization Options:
- Adjust sweetness by varying the amount of sweetener used in the recipe.

Important Notes:
- Do not overmix the dough to ensure scones remain light and tender.

Nutritional Value: (Per Scone)
- Calories: ~220
- Total Fat: 18g
- Carbohydrates: 7g
- Fiber: 4g
- Protein: 7g

Almond Flour Biscotti

Preparation Time: 20 minutes + cooling time **Cooking Time:** 35-40 minutes **Servings:** 12 biscotti

Ingredients:
- 2 cups almond flour
- 1/3 cup erythritol or sweetener of choice
- 1 teaspoon baking powder
- Pinch of salt
- 2 large eggs
- 1 teaspoon vanilla extract
- 1/2 cup chopped sugar-free dark chocolate or sugar-free chocolate chips
- 1/2 cup chopped almonds or hazelnuts (optional)

Directions:
1. Preheat the oven to 325°F (160°C) and line a baking sheet with parchment paper.
2. In a mixing bowl, combine almond flour, erythritol, baking powder, and salt.
3. In another bowl, whisk together eggs and vanilla extract.
4. Mix the wet ingredients into the dry ingredients until a dough forms.
5. Fold in chopped chocolate and nuts if using, until evenly distributed.
6. Divide the dough in half and shape each half into a log on the prepared baking sheet.
7. Bake for 20-25 minutes until the logs are lightly golden and firm to the touch.
8. Remove from the oven and let them cool for 10-15 minutes.
9. Using a sharp knife, slice the logs diagonally into 1-inch wide biscotti.
10. Place the biscotti cut-side down on the baking sheet and bake for an additional 10-15 minutes until crisp.
11. Cool completely before serving or storing in an airtight container.

Recipe Variations:
- Add a teaspoon of orange zest or almond extract for enhanced flavors.
- Use different nuts or seeds for texture variations.

Topping Options:
- Drizzle with melted sugar-free chocolate or dip in coffee for serving.

Customization Options:
- Adjust sweetness or add spices like cinnamon or nutmeg to suit taste preferences.

Important Notes:
- Ensure biscotti slices are completely cooled and crisp before storing to maintain their texture.

Nutritional Value: (Per Biscotti)
- Calories: ~140
- Total Fat: 12g
- Carbohydrates: 5g
- Fiber: 2g
- Protein: 5g

Almond Flour Macarons

Preparation Time: 45 minutes **Cooking Time:** 12-15 minutes **Resting Time:** 30-60 minutes **Servings:** ~20 macarons

Ingredients:
- 1 1/2 cups almond flour
- 1 3/4 cups powdered erythritol or sweetener of choice
- 3 large egg whites, room temperature
- Pinch of cream of tartar
- 1/4 cup erythritol (for meringue)
- Food coloring (optional)
- Sugar-free ganache or buttercream for filling

Directions:
1. Line two baking sheets with parchment paper and preheat the oven to 300°F (150°C).
2. In a food processor, pulse almond flour and powdered sweetener until fine.
3. In a clean, dry mixing bowl, beat egg whites and cream of tartar until foamy.
4. Gradually add erythritol for the meringue, beating until stiff peaks form.
5. Gently fold the almond flour mixture into the meringue until combined and glossy.
6. Add food coloring if desired and continue folding until the color is uniform.
7. Transfer the batter to a piping bag fitted with a round tip and pipe small circles onto the prepared baking sheets.
8. Tap the baking sheets gently to release any air bubbles and let the macarons sit at room temperature for 30-60 minutes to form a skin.
9. Bake for 12-15 minutes, rotating the sheets halfway through, until the macarons have formed "feet" and are set.
10. Remove from the oven and let them cool completely before filling with ganache or buttercream.

Recipe Variations:
- Experiment with different flavors for the filling like raspberry, chocolate, or vanilla.
- Add ground nuts or spices to the batter for unique macaron varieties.

Topping Options:
- Sprinkle with edible glitter or dust with powdered erythritol for decoration.

Customization Options:
- Adjust the sweetness or experiment with colors for creative presentations.

Important Notes:
- Macaron batter should be thick but flow easily; avoid overmixing to maintain proper consistency.
- Ensure macarons are completely cooled before filling to prevent melting of the filling.

Nutritional Value: (Per Macaron, without filling)
- Calories: ~60
- Total Fat: 5g
- Carbohydrates: 2g
- Fiber: 1g
- Protein: 2g

Almond Flour Tartlets

Preparation Time: 30 minutes **Cooking Time:** 15-18 minutes **Servings:** 12 tartlets

Ingredients:
- 2 cups almond flour
- 1/4 cup coconut flour
- 1/4 cup erythritol or sweetener of choice
- 1/4 teaspoon salt
- 1/4 cup melted coconut oil or butter
- 1 large egg
- Sugar-free fruit preserves or lemon curd for filling

Directions:
1. Preheat the oven to 350°F (175°C) and grease a muffin tin or tartlet pans.
2. In a mixing bowl, combine almond flour, coconut flour, erythritol, and salt.
3. Stir in melted coconut oil or butter and the egg until a dough forms.
4. Divide the dough into 12 portions and press each portion evenly into the prepared tartlet pans.
5. Prick the bottoms of the tartlet crusts with a fork and bake for 15-18 minutes until golden brown.
6. Allow the tartlet crusts to cool completely before removing them from the pans.
7. Fill each tartlet with a spoonful of sugar-free fruit preserves or lemon curd.

Recipe Variations:
- Add a layer of whipped cream or a dollop of mascarpone cheese before adding the fruit filling.
- Top with fresh berries or a sprinkle of powdered erythritol for garnish.

Topping Options:
- Dust with powdered erythritol or a drizzle of sugar-free glaze for decoration.

Customization Options:
- Experiment with different fillings or add spices like cinnamon or nutmeg to the crust.

Important Notes:
- Ensure tartlet crusts are completely cooled before filling to avoid soggy bottoms.

Nutritional Value: (Per Tartlet, without filling)
- Calories: ~150
- Total Fat: 12g
- Carbohydrates: 5g
- Fiber: 3g
- Protein: 6g

Almond Flour Muffins

Preparation Time: 15 minutes **Cooking Time:** 20-25 minutes **Servings:** 12 muffins

Ingredients:
- 2 cups almond flour
- 1/3 cup erythritol or sweetener of choice
- 1 teaspoon baking powder
- 1/2 teaspoon baking soda
- Pinch of salt
- 3 large eggs
- 1/2 cup unsweetened applesauce or mashed ripe bananas
- 1/4 cup almond milk or any milk of choice
- 1 teaspoon vanilla extract
- 1/2 cup fresh berries or sugar-free chocolate chips (optional)

Directions:
1. Preheat the oven to 350°F (175°C) and line a muffin tin with paper liners.
2. In a large bowl, whisk together almond flour, erythritol, baking powder, baking soda, and salt.
3. In another bowl, beat the eggs, then add applesauce or mashed bananas, almond milk, and vanilla extract. Mix well.
4. Combine the wet and dry ingredients until just incorporated. Do not overmix.
5. Gently fold in fresh berries or sugar-free chocolate chips if using.
6. Spoon the batter evenly into the muffin cups, filling each about 2/3 full.
7. Bake for 20-25 minutes until a toothpick inserted into the center comes out clean.
8. Allow the muffins to cool in the pan for a few minutes before transferring them to a wire rack to cool completely.

Recipe Variations:
- Add a tablespoon of lemon zest or cinnamon for added flavor.
- Mix in chopped nuts or seeds for added texture.

Topping Options:
- Sprinkle with a dusting of powdered erythritol or add a dollop of sugar-free jam on top.

Customization Options:
- Adjust sweetness by varying the amount of sweetener used in the recipe.

Important Notes:
- Do not overmix the batter to keep the muffins light and fluffy.
- Ensure the muffins are completely cooled before storing.

Nutritional Value: (Per Muffin)
- Calories: ~130
- Total Fat: 10g
- Carbohydrates: 6g
- Fiber: 3g
- Protein: 5g

Almond Flour Brownies

Preparation Time: 15 minutes **Cooking Time:** 25-30 minutes **Servings:** 16 brownies

Ingredients:
- 2 cups almond flour
- 1/2 cup unsweetened cocoa powder
- 1/2 teaspoon baking soda
- 1/2 teaspoon salt
- 1/2 cup melted coconut oil or butter
- 1/2 cup erythritol or sweetener of choice
- 3 large eggs
- 1 teaspoon vanilla extract
- 1/2 cup sugar-free chocolate chips (optional)
- Chopped nuts or seeds for topping (optional)

Directions:
1. Preheat the oven to 350°F (175°C) and line an 8x8-inch baking pan with parchment paper.
2. In a bowl, whisk together almond flour, cocoa powder, baking soda, and salt.
3. In another bowl, mix melted coconut oil or butter with erythritol, eggs, and vanilla extract until well combined.
4. Combine the wet and dry ingredients, stirring until smooth. Fold in sugar-free chocolate chips if using.
5. Pour the batter into the prepared baking pan, spreading it evenly.
6. Sprinkle chopped nuts or seeds on top if desired.
7. Bake for 25-30 minutes or until a toothpick inserted into the center comes out with a few moist crumbs.
8. Allow the brownies to cool completely in the pan before slicing into squares.

Recipe Variations:
- Add a tablespoon of instant coffee for a mocha-flavored twist.
- Mix in chopped walnuts or pecans for added crunch.

Topping Options:
- Dust with powdered erythritol or cocoa powder for decoration.

Customization Options:
- Adjust sweetness or add extracts like mint or almond for different flavors.

Important Notes:
- Ensure the brownies are completely cooled before cutting for clean slices.
- Store in an airtight container at room temperature or in the fridge.

Nutritional Value: (Per Brownie)
- Calories: ~160
- Total Fat: 14g
- Carbohydrates: 6g
- Fiber: 3g
- Protein: 5g

ALMOND FLOUR CRUSTS

Almond flour crusts work for both savory quiches and sweet tarts. They add a nutty flavor to any filling.

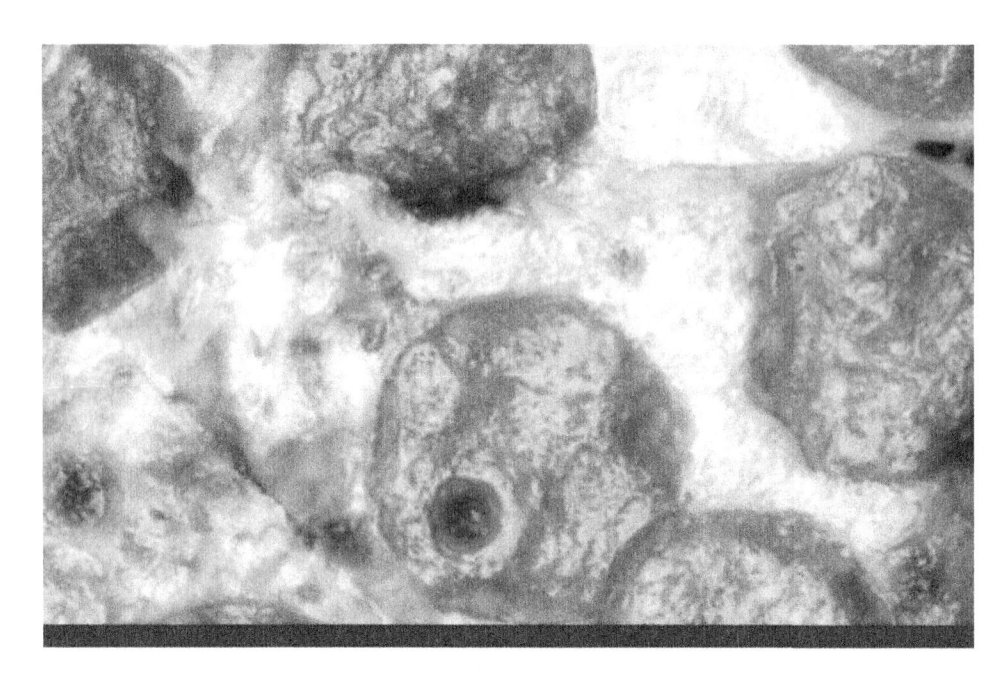

Almond Flour Pie Crust

Preparation Time: 10 minutes **Cooking Time:** 10-12 minutes (for pre-baking, if required) **Servings:** 1 standard pie crust

Ingredients:
- 1 1/2 cups almond flour
- 1/4 cup melted coconut oil or butter
- Pinch of salt
- 1 tablespoon sweetener (optional, for sweet pies)
- 1 egg (for binding, optional)

Directions:
1. In a mixing bowl, combine almond flour, melted coconut oil or butter, salt, and sweetener if making a sweet pie crust.
2. Mix the ingredients until a dough forms. If needed, add an egg to bind the mixture better.
3. Press the dough evenly into a pie dish to form the crust.
4. If pre-baking, preheat the oven to 350°F (175°C). Dock the crust with a fork and bake for 10-12 minutes until lightly golden.
5. Proceed with your pie recipe as directed.

Recipe Variations:
- Add a teaspoon of cinnamon for a flavorful twist in sweet pie crusts.
- Use a combination of almond and coconut flour for a slightly different texture.

Customization Options:
- Adjust sweetness or add spices according to the type of pie being made.
- For a flakier crust, chill the dough before pressing it into the pie dish.

Important Notes:
- Ensure the crust is properly pre-baked for recipes that require a pre-baked crust.

Nutritional Value: (Per Pie Crust)
- Calories: ~800 (entire crust)
- Total Fat: 72g
- Carbohydrates: 12g
- Fiber: 6g
- Protein: 24g

Almond Flour Tart Crust

Preparation Time: 15 minutes **Cooking Time:** 10-12 minutes (for pre-baking, if required) **Servings:** 1 standard tart crust

Ingredients:
- 1 1/2 cups almond flour
- 1/4 cup melted coconut oil or butter
- Pinch of salt
- 1 tablespoon sweetener (optional, for sweet tarts)
- 1 egg (for binding, optional)

Directions:
1. In a bowl, mix almond flour, melted coconut oil or butter, salt, and sweetener if making a sweet tart crust.
2. Combine the ingredients until a dough forms. Add an egg if necessary for better binding.
3. Press the dough evenly into a tart pan to form the crust.
4. If pre-baking, preheat the oven to 350°F (175°C). Dock the crust with a fork and bake for 10-12 minutes until lightly golden.
5. Use as a base for your tart recipes.

Recipe Variations:
- Substitute some almond flour with hazelnut or walnut flour for a nuttier flavor.
- Add lemon zest for a citrusy note in sweet tart crusts.

Topping Options:
- Typically, tart crusts are filled with various fillings as part of the tart recipe.

Customization Options:
- Adjust sweetness or incorporate different spices based on the tart's filling.

Important Notes:
- Ensure the tart crust is adequately pre-baked before adding fillings that require a pre-baked crust.

Nutritional Value: (Per Tart Crust)
- Calories: ~800 (entire crust)
- Total Fat: 72g
- Carbohydrates: 12g
- Fiber: 6g
- Protein: 24g

Almond Flour Quiche Crust

Preparation Time: 10 minutes **Cooking Time:** 10-12 minutes (for pre-baking, if required) **Servings:** 1 standard quiche crust

Ingredients:
- 1 1/2 cups almond flour
- 1/4 cup melted coconut oil or butter
- Pinch of salt
- 1 tablespoon sweetener (optional)
- 1 egg (for binding, optional)

Directions:
1. In a bowl, mix almond flour, melted coconut oil or butter, salt, and sweetener if making a sweet quiche crust.
2. Combine the ingredients until a dough forms. Add an egg if needed for better binding.
3. Press the dough evenly into a quiche dish to form the crust.
4. If pre-baking, preheat the oven to 350°F (175°C). Dock the crust with a fork and bake for 10-12 minutes until lightly golden.
5. Proceed with your quiche recipe as directed.

Recipe Variations:
- Incorporate herbs like thyme or rosemary into the crust for added flavor.
- Use a mix of almond and coconut flour for a slightly different texture.

Topping Options:
- The quiche crust is typically filled with a variety of savory fillings.

Customization Options:
- Adjust the saltiness or add different herbs according to the quiche's filling.

Important Notes:
- Ensure the quiche crust is properly pre-baked if your quiche recipe requires a pre-baked crust.

Nutritional Value: (Per Quiche Crust)
- Calories: ~800 (entire crust)
- Total Fat: 72g
- Carbohydrates: 12g
- Fiber: 6g
- Protein: 24g

Almond Flour Cheesecake Crust

Preparation Time: 10 minutes **Cooking Time:** 10-12 minutes (for pre-baking, if required) **Servings:** 1 standard cheesecake crust

Ingredients:
- 1 1/2 cups almond flour
- 1/4 cup melted coconut oil or butter
- Pinch of salt
- 1 tablespoon sweetener (optional, for sweeter crusts)
- 1 egg (for binding, optional)

Directions:
1. In a bowl, mix almond flour, melted coconut oil or butter, salt, and sweetener if making a sweeter cheesecake crust.
2. Combine the ingredients until a dough forms. Add an egg if required for better binding.
3. Press the dough evenly into the base of a springform pan to form the crust.
4. If pre-baking, preheat the oven to 350°F (175°C). Dock the crust with a fork and bake for 10-12 minutes until lightly golden.
5. Proceed with your cheesecake recipe as directed.

Recipe Variations:
- Add a teaspoon of lemon zest for a citrusy note in sweet cheesecake crusts.
- Incorporate ground nuts like pecans or hazelnuts for a nuttier flavor.

Topping Options:
- The cheesecake crust is typically topped with the cheesecake filling and additional toppings or sauces.

Customization Options:
- Adjust sweetness or incorporate different spices based on the cheesecake's flavor profile.

Important Notes:
- Ensure the cheesecake crust is properly pre-baked for recipes that require a pre-baked crust.

Nutritional Value: (Per Cheesecake Crust)
- Calories: ~800 (entire crust)
- Total Fat: 72g
- Carbohydrates: 12g
- Fiber: 6g
- Protein: 24g

Almond Flour Galette Crust

Preparation Time: 10 minutes **Cooking Time:** 10-12 minutes (for pre-baking, if required) **Servings:** 1 standard galette crust

Ingredients:
- 1 1/2 cups almond flour
- 1/4 cup melted coconut oil or butter
- Pinch of salt
- 1 tablespoon sweetener (optional, for sweet galettes)
- 1 egg (for binding, optional)

Directions:
1. In a bowl, mix almond flour, melted coconut oil or butter, salt, and sweetener if making a sweet galette crust.
2. Combine the ingredients until a dough forms. Add an egg if needed for better binding.
3. Roll out the dough on a piece of parchment paper into a circle, about 1/8 inch thick.
4. Transfer the rolled-out dough with the parchment paper onto a baking sheet.
5. If pre-baking, preheat the oven to 350°F (175°C). Dock the crust with a fork and bake for 10-12 minutes until lightly golden.
6. Use as the base for your galette recipe.

Recipe Variations:
- Add a teaspoon of vanilla extract or ground spices like cinnamon for a flavor boost.
- Incorporate finely grated lemon zest for a citrusy hint in sweet galette crusts.

Topping Options:
- Galette crusts are typically filled with fruits, jams, or savory fillings before folding and baking.

Customization Options:
- Adjust sweetness or add different spices according to the galette's filling.

Important Notes:
- Ensure the galette crust is adequately pre-baked if your galette recipe requires a pre-baked crust.

Nutritional Value: (Per Galette Crust)
- Calories: ~800 (entire crust)
- Total Fat: 72g
- Carbohydrates: 12g
- Fiber: 6g
- Protein: 24g

Almond Flour Pizza Crust

Preparation Time: 15 minutes **Cooking Time:** 20-25 minutes **Servings:** 1 standard pizza crust

Ingredients:
- 2 cups almond flour
- 2 tablespoons psyllium husk powder
- 1 teaspoon baking powder
- 1/2 teaspoon salt
- 2 tablespoons olive oil
- 2 large eggs
- 1/4 cup water

Directions:
1. Preheat the oven to 375°F (190°C) and line a baking sheet with parchment paper.
2. In a bowl, mix almond flour, psyllium husk powder, baking powder, and salt.
3. Add olive oil and eggs to the dry ingredients and mix well.
4. Gradually add water while stirring until a dough forms.
5. Place the dough on the prepared baking sheet and press it out evenly into a round pizza shape.
6. Bake the crust for 15 minutes until it starts to firm up.
7. Remove from the oven, add desired toppings, and bake for an additional 5-10 minutes until toppings are cooked and crust is golden brown.

Recipe Variations:
- Incorporate Italian herbs or garlic powder into the dough for a seasoned crust.
- Use a blend of almond and coconut flour for a slightly different texture.

Topping Options:
- Top the pizza crust with desired sauce, cheese, vegetables, meats, or other toppings of choice.

Customization Options:
- Adjust the thickness of the crust based on personal preference.
- Experiment with different seasoning blends for varied flavors.

Important Notes:
- Ensure the crust is baked until golden and firm before adding toppings to prevent sogginess.

Nutritional Value: (Per Pizza Crust)
- Calories: ~1300 (entire crust)
- Total Fat: 100g
- Carbohydrates: 48g
- Fiber: 24g
- Protein: 48g

Almond Flour Shortcrust for Tarts

Preparation Time: 15 minutes **Cooking Time**: 10-12 minutes (for pre-baking, if required) **Servings**: 1 standard tart crust

Ingredients:
- 1 1/2 cups almond flour
- 1/4 cup melted coconut oil or butter
- Pinch of salt
- 1 tablespoon sweetener (optional, for sweet tart crusts)
- 1 egg (for binding, optional)

Directions:
1. In a bowl, mix almond flour, melted coconut oil or butter, salt, and sweetener if making a sweet tart crust.
2. Combine the ingredients until a dough forms. Add an egg if needed for better binding.
3. Press the dough evenly into a tart pan to form the crust.
4. If pre-baking, preheat the oven to 350°F (175°C). Dock the crust with a fork and bake for 10-12 minutes until lightly golden.
5. Use as the base for your tart recipes.

Recipe Variations:
- Add a teaspoon of lemon zest for a citrusy note in sweet tart crusts.
- Incorporate ground nuts like pecans or hazelnuts for a nuttier flavor.

Topping Options:
- The tart crust is typically filled with various sweet or savory fillings based on the tart recipe.

Customization Options:
- Adjust sweetness or incorporate different spices based on the tart's filling.

Important Notes:
- Ensure the tart crust is adequately pre-baked before adding fillings that require a pre-baked crust.

Nutritional Value: (Per Tart Crust)
- Calories: ~800 (entire crust)
- Total Fat: 72g
- Carbohydrates: 12g
- Fiber: 6g
- Protein: 24g

ALMOND FLOUR CAKES

Almond flour cakes are moist and delicious, especially with frosting or fruit toppings. They're gluten-free too!

Almond Flour Vanilla Cake

Preparation Time: 15 minutes **Cooking Time:** 25-30 minutes **Servings:** 8-10 slices

Ingredients:
- 2 cups almond flour
- 1/2 cup granulated sugar or sweetener of choice
- 1/4 cup melted butter or coconut oil
- 4 eggs
- 1/4 cup almond milk or any milk of choice
- 2 teaspoons baking powder
- 1 teaspoon vanilla extract
- Pinch of salt

Directions:

1. Preheat the oven to 350°F (175°C) and grease a cake pan.
2. In a mixing bowl, combine almond flour, sugar, baking powder, and salt.
3. In another bowl, whisk together melted butter, eggs, almond milk, and vanilla extract.
4. Gradually add the wet ingredients to the dry ingredients, mixing until well combined.
5. Pour the batter into the prepared cake pan and spread evenly.
6. Bake for 25-30 minutes or until a toothpick inserted into the center comes out clean.
7. Let the cake cool in the pan for 10 minutes, then transfer to a wire rack to cool completely.

Recipe Variations:
- Add a tablespoon of lemon zest for a citrusy flavor.
- Use maple syrup or honey as a sweetener for a different taste profile.

Topping Options:
- Frost with vanilla buttercream or whipped cream.
- Top with fresh berries or sliced almonds for decoration.

Customization Options:
- Adjust sweetness or add spices like cinnamon for variation.

Important Notes:
- Ensure the cake is completely cooled before frosting to prevent melting of the icing.

Nutritional Value: (Per Slice)
- Calories: ~250
- Total Fat: 20g
- Carbohydrates: 10g
- Fiber: 3g
- Protein: 8g

Almond Flour Chocolate Cake

Preparation Time: 20 minutes **Cooking Time:** 30-35 minutes **Servings:** 8-10 slices

Ingredients:
- 2 cups almond flour
- 1/2 cup cocoa powder
- 1/2 cup granulated sugar or sweetener of choice
- 1/4 cup melted butter or coconut oil
- 4 eggs
- 1/4 cup almond milk or any milk of choice
- 2 teaspoons baking powder
- 1 teaspoon vanilla extract
- Pinch of salt

Directions:
1. Preheat the oven to 350°F (175°C) and grease a cake pan.
2. In a mixing bowl, combine almond flour, cocoa powder, sugar, baking powder, and salt.
3. In another bowl, whisk together melted butter, eggs, almond milk, and vanilla extract.
4. Gradually add the wet ingredients to the dry ingredients, mixing until well combined.
5. Pour the batter into the prepared cake pan and spread evenly.
6. Bake for 30-35 minutes or until a toothpick inserted into the center comes out clean.
7. Let the cake cool in the pan for 10 minutes, then transfer to a wire rack to cool completely.

Recipe Variations:
- Fold in sugar-free chocolate chips for added richness.
- Substitute part of the almond flour with hazelnut flour for a nutty taste.

Topping Options:
- Frost with chocolate ganache or dust with powdered sugar.
- Garnish with sliced strawberries or raspberries.

Customization Options:
- Adjust sweetness or experiment with different types of cocoa powder for varied intensities.

Important Notes:
- Ensure the cake is completely cooled before applying frosting or toppings.

Nutritional Value: (Per Slice)
- Calories: ~280
- Total Fat: 22g
- Carbohydrates: 12g
- Fiber: 4g
- Protein: 9g

Almond Flour Lemon Cake

Preparation Time: 20 minutes **Cooking Time:** 25-30 minutes **Servings:** 8-10 slices

Ingredients:
- 2 cups almond flour
- 1/2 cup granulated sugar or sweetener of choice
- 1/4 cup melted butter or coconut oil
- 4 eggs
- 1/4 cup lemon juice
- Zest of 1-2 lemons
- 2 teaspoons baking powder
- 1 teaspoon vanilla extract
- Pinch of salt

Directions:
1. Preheat the oven to 350°F (175°C) and grease a cake pan.
2. In a mixing bowl, combine almond flour, sugar, baking powder, and salt.
3. In another bowl, whisk together melted butter, eggs, lemon juice, lemon zest, and vanilla extract.
4. Gradually add the wet ingredients to the dry ingredients, mixing until well combined.
5. Pour the batter into the prepared cake pan and spread evenly.
6. Bake for 25-30 minutes or until a toothpick inserted into the center comes out clean.
7. Let the cake cool in the pan for 10 minutes, then transfer to a wire rack to cool completely.

Recipe Variations:
- Substitute part of the lemon juice with orange juice for a citrus blend.
- Add a tablespoon of poppy seeds for a lemon-poppy seed cake.

Topping Options:
- Drizzle with a lemon glaze or top with a light cream cheese frosting.
- Garnish with lemon slices or zest.

Customization Options:
- Adjust sweetness or increase lemon zest for a tangier flavor.

Important Notes:
- Ensure the cake is completely cooled before applying frosting or glaze.

Nutritional Value: (Per Slice)
- Calories: ~260
- Total Fat: 20g
- Carbohydrates: 12g
- Fiber: 4g
- Protein: 9g

Almond Flour Carrot Cake

Preparation Time: 25 minutes **Cooking Time:** 30-35 minutes **Servings:** 8-10 slices

Ingredients:
- 2 cups almond flour
- ½ cup granulated sugar or sweetener of choice
- 1/4 cup melted butter or coconut oil
- 4 eggs
- 1 cup grated carrots
- 1/4 cup chopped walnuts or pecans (optional)
- 2 teaspoons baking powder
- 1 teaspoon cinnamon
- 1/2 teaspoon nutmeg
- 1 teaspoon vanilla extract
- Pinch of salt

Directions:
1. Preheat the oven to 350°F (175°C) and grease a cake pan.
2. In a mixing bowl, combine almond flour, sugar, baking powder, cinnamon, nutmeg, and salt.
3. In another bowl, whisk together melted butter, eggs, vanilla extract, grated carrots, and chopped nuts if using.
4. Gradually add the wet ingredients to the dry ingredients, mixing until well combined.
5. Pour the batter into the prepared cake pan and spread evenly.
6. Bake for 30-35 minutes or until a toothpick inserted into the center comes out clean.
7. Let the cake cool in the pan for 10 minutes, then transfer to a wire rack to cool completely.

Recipe Variations:
- Fold in shredded coconut for added texture.
- Substitute some almond flour with coconut flour for a lighter texture.

Topping Options:
- Frost with cream cheese frosting or a vanilla glaze.
- Garnish with shredded carrots or a sprinkle of cinnamon.

Customization Options:
- Adjust sweetness or add raisins for extra sweetness and texture.

Important Notes:
- Ensure the cake is completely cooled before applying frosting or glaze.

Nutritional Value: (Per Slice)
- Calories: ~270
- Total Fat: 21g
- Carbohydrates: 13g
- Fiber: 4g
- Protein: 9g

Almond Flour Orange Cake

Preparation Time: 20 minutes **Cooking Time**: 25-30 minutes **Servings**: 8-10 slices

Ingredients:
- 2 cups almond flour
- 1/2 cup granulated sugar or sweetener of choice
- 1/4 cup melted butter or coconut oil
- 4 eggs
- Zest of 2 oranges
- 1/4 cup orange juice
- 2 teaspoons baking powder
- 1 teaspoon vanilla extract
- Pinch of salt

Directions:
1. Preheat the oven to 350°F (175°C) and grease a cake pan.
2. In a mixing bowl, combine almond flour, sugar, baking powder, and salt.
3. In another bowl, whisk together melted butter, eggs, orange zest, orange juice, and vanilla extract.
4. Gradually add the wet ingredients to the dry ingredients, mixing until well combined.
5. Pour the batter into the prepared cake pan and spread evenly.
6. Bake for 25-30 minutes or until a toothpick inserted into the center comes out clean.
7. Let the cake cool in the pan for 10 minutes, then transfer to a wire rack to cool completely.

Recipe Variations:
- Substitute part of the orange juice with lemon juice for a citrus blend.
- Add a tablespoon of Grand Marnier or orange liqueur for a hint of sophistication.

Topping Options:
- Drizzle with an orange glaze or dust with powdered sugar.
- Garnish with orange slices or zest.

Customization Options:
- Adjust sweetness or increase orange zest for a stronger citrus flavor.

Important Notes:
- Ensure the cake is completely cooled before applying frosting or glaze.

Nutritional Value: (Per Slice)
- Calories: ~270
- Total Fat: 20g
- Carbohydrates: 12g
- Fiber: 4g
- Protein: 9g

Almond Flour Coconut Cake

Preparation Time: 20 minutes **Cooking Time:** 30-35 minutes **Servings:** 8-10 slices

Ingredients:
- 2 cups almond flour
- 1/2 cup granulated sugar or sweetener of choice
- 1/4 cup melted butter or coconut oil
- 4 eggs
- 1/2 cup shredded coconut (unsweetened)
- 2 teaspoons baking powder
- 1 teaspoon vanilla extract
- Pinch of salt

Directions:
1. Preheat the oven to 350°F (175°C) and grease a cake pan.
2. In a mixing bowl, combine almond flour, sugar, baking powder, shredded coconut, and salt.
3. In another bowl, whisk together melted butter, eggs, and vanilla extract.
4. Gradually add the wet ingredients to the dry ingredients, mixing until well combined.
5. Pour the batter into the prepared cake pan and spread evenly.
6. Bake for 30-35 minutes or until a toothpick inserted into the center comes out clean.
7. Let the cake cool in the pan for 10 minutes, then transfer to a wire rack to cool completely.

Recipe Variations:
- Add a tablespoon of rum or coconut extract for a stronger coconut flavor.
- Substitute part of the almond flour with coconut flour for added coconut essence.

Topping Options:
- Frost with coconut cream or a vanilla glaze.
- Garnish with toasted coconut flakes or fresh berries.

Customization Options:
- Adjust sweetness or add chopped nuts for a crunchy texture.

Important Notes:
- Ensure the cake is completely cooled before applying frosting or glaze.

Nutritional Value: (Per Slice)
- Calories: ~260
- Total Fat: 20g
- Carbohydrates: 12g
- Fiber: 4g
- Protein: 9g

Almond Flour Raspberry Cake

Preparation Time: 20 minutes **Cooking Time**: 30-35 minutes **Servings**: 8-10 slices

Ingredients:
- 2 cups almond flour
- 1/2 cup granulated sugar or sweetener of choice
- 1/4 cup melted butter or coconut oil
- 4 eggs
- 1 cup fresh raspberries
- 2 teaspoons baking powder
- 1 teaspoon vanilla extract
- Pinch of salt

Directions:
1. Preheat the oven to 350°F (175°C) and grease a cake pan.
2. In a mixing bowl, combine almond flour, sugar, baking powder, and salt.
3. In another bowl, whisk together melted butter, eggs, and vanilla extract.
4. Gradually add the wet ingredients to the dry ingredients, mixing until well combined.
5. Gently fold in the fresh raspberries into the batter.
6. Pour the batter into the prepared cake pan and spread evenly.
7. Bake for 30-35 minutes or until a toothpick inserted into the center comes out clean.
8. Let the cake cool in the pan for 10 minutes, then transfer to a wire rack to cool completely.

Recipe Variations:
- Use frozen raspberries if fresh ones are not available.
- Incorporate raspberry extract for a more intense flavor.

Topping Options:
- Frost with a raspberry buttercream or a simple glaze.
- Garnish with additional fresh raspberries or a dusting of powdered sugar.

Customization Options:
- Adjust sweetness or add a hint of lemon zest for an added zing.

Important Notes:
- Ensure the cake is completely cooled before applying frosting or glaze.

Nutritional Value: (Per Slice)
- Calories: ~240
- Total Fat: 18g
- Carbohydrates: 12g
- Fiber: 4g
- Protein: 8g

Almond Flour Coffee Cake

Preparation Time: 20 minutes **Cooking Time:** 35-40 minutes **Servings:** 8-10 slices

Ingredients:
- 2 cups almond flour
- 1/2 cup granulated sugar or sweetener of choice
- 1/4 cup melted butter or coconut oil
- 4 eggs
- 1/4 cup brewed coffee, cooled
- 2 teaspoons baking powder
- 1 teaspoon vanilla extract
- Pinch of salt

Directions:
1. Preheat the oven to 350°F (175°C) and grease a cake pan.
2. In a mixing bowl, combine almond flour, sugar, baking powder, and salt.
3. In another bowl, whisk together melted butter, eggs, brewed coffee, and vanilla extract.
4. Gradually add the wet ingredients to the dry ingredients, mixing until well combined.
5. Pour the batter into the prepared cake pan and spread evenly.
6. Bake for 35-40 minutes or until a toothpick inserted into the center comes out clean.
7. Let the cake cool in the pan for 10 minutes, then transfer to a wire rack to cool completely.

Recipe Variations:
- Add a teaspoon of cinnamon or nutmeg for a spiced coffee flavor.
- Incorporate chopped nuts like walnuts or pecans for added texture.

Topping Options:
- Sprinkle with a cinnamon-sugar mixture or a streusel topping.
- Serve with a dollop of whipped cream or a drizzle of caramel.

Customization Options:
- Adjust sweetness or experiment with different types of coffee for varied tastes.

Important Notes:
- Ensure the cake is completely cooled before slicing.

Nutritional Value: (Per Slice)
- Calories: ~250
- Total Fat: 20g
- Carbohydrates: 12g
- Fiber: 4g
- Protein: 8g

ALMOND FLOUR CUPCAKES

These almond flour cupcakes are soft and topped with creamy frosting. A guilt-free treat for any celebration.

Almond Flour Chocolate Cupcakes

Preparation Time: 15 minutes **Cooking Time:** 20-25 minutes **Servings:** 12 cupcakes

Ingredients:
- 2 cups almond flour
- 1/2 cup granulated sugar or sweetener of choice
- 1/4 cup melted butter or coconut oil
- 4 eggs
- 1/4 cup almond milk or any milk of choice
- 1/4 cup unsweetened cocoa powder
- 2 teaspoons baking powder
- 1 teaspoon vanilla extract
- Pinch of salt

Directions:
1. Preheat the oven to 350°F (175°C) and line a muffin tin with cupcake liners.
2. In a mixing bowl, combine almond flour, sugar, cocoa powder, baking powder, and salt.
3. In another bowl, whisk together melted butter, eggs, almond milk, and vanilla extract.
4. Gradually add the wet ingredients to the dry ingredients, mixing until well combined.
5. Pour the batter into the cupcake liners, filling each about two-thirds full.
6. Bake for 20-25 minutes or until a toothpick inserted into the center comes out clean.
7. Let the cupcakes cool in the tin for 5 minutes, then transfer to a wire rack to cool completely.

Recipe Variations:
- Add chocolate chips for an extra burst of chocolate flavor.
- Substitute almond milk with coconut milk for a richer taste.

Topping Options:
- Frost with chocolate ganache or a chocolate buttercream.
- Garnish with chocolate shavings or a dusting of cocoa powder.

Customization Options:
- Adjust sweetness or experiment with different types of cocoa powder for varied intensities.

Important Notes:
- Ensure the cupcakes are completely cooled before frosting.

Nutritional Value: (Per Cupcake)
- Calories: ~210
- Total Fat: 17g
- Carbohydrates: 8.5g
- Fiber: 2.5g
- Protein: 6.5g

Almond Flour Lemon Cupcakes

Preparation Time: 15 minutes **Cooking Time:** 20-25 minutes **Servings:** 12 cupcakes

Ingredients:
- 2 cups almond flour
- 1/2 cup granulated sugar or sweetener of choice
- 1/4 cup melted butter or coconut oil
- 4 eggs
- Zest of 2 lemons
- 1/4 cup fresh lemon juice
- 2 teaspoons baking powder
- 1 teaspoon vanilla extract
- Pinch of salt

Directions:
1. Preheat the oven to 350°F (175°C) and line a muffin tin with cupcake liners.
2. In a mixing bowl, combine almond flour, sugar, baking powder, and salt.
3. In another bowl, whisk together melted butter, eggs, lemon zest, lemon juice, and vanilla extract.
4. Gradually add the wet ingredients to the dry ingredients, mixing until well combined.
5. Pour the batter into the cupcake liners, filling each about two-thirds full.
6. Bake for 20-25 minutes or until a toothpick inserted into the center comes out clean.
7. Let the cupcakes cool in the tin for 5 minutes, then transfer to a wire rack to cool completely.

Recipe Variations:
- Add a teaspoon of poppy seeds for a lemon-poppy seed variation.
- Substitute part of the almond flour with coconut flour for a lighter texture.

Topping Options:
- Frost with a lemon glaze or a light cream cheese frosting.
- Garnish with a twist of lemon zest or a slice of lemon.

Customization Options:
- Adjust sweetness or increase lemon zest for a tangier flavor.

Important Notes:
- Ensure the cupcakes are completely cooled before frosting.

Nutritional Value: (Per Cupcake)
- Calories: ~200
- Total Fat: 16g
- Carbohydrates: 8g
- Fiber: 2g
- Protein: 6g

Almond Flour Pumpkin Cupcakes

Preparation Time: 15 minutes **Cooking Time:** 20-25 minutes **Servings:** 12 cupcakes

Ingredients:
- 2 cups almond flour
- 1/2 cup granulated sugar or sweetener of choice
- 1/4 cup melted butter or coconut oil
- 4 eggs
- 1/2 cup pumpkin puree
- 1 teaspoon pumpkin pie spice (or a mix of cinnamon, nutmeg, and cloves)
- 2 teaspoons baking powder
- 1 teaspoon vanilla extract
- Pinch of salt

Directions:
1. Preheat the oven to 350°F (175°C) and line a muffin tin with cupcake liners.
2. In a mixing bowl, combine almond flour, sugar, pumpkin pie spice, baking powder, and salt.
3. In another bowl, whisk together melted butter, eggs, pumpkin puree, and vanilla extract.
4. Gradually add the wet ingredients to the dry ingredients, mixing until well combined.
5. Pour the batter into the cupcake liners, filling each about two-thirds full.
6. Bake for 20-25 minutes or until a toothpick inserted into the center comes out clean.
7. Let the cupcakes cool in the tin for 5 minutes, then transfer to a wire rack to cool completely.

Recipe Variations:
- Add chopped nuts or raisins for added texture.
- Incorporate a cream cheese swirl for a pumpkin-cream cheese variation.

Topping Options:
- Frost with cream cheese frosting or a maple glaze.
- Sprinkle with pumpkin pie spice or chopped nuts for decoration.

Customization Options:
- Adjust sweetness or increase pumpkin pie spice for more warmth.

Important Notes:
- Ensure the cupcakes are completely cooled before frosting.

Nutritional Value: (Per Cupcake)
- Calories: ~190
- Total Fat: 15g
- Carbohydrates: 7g
- Fiber: 2g
- Protein: 6g

(

Almond Flour Red Velvet Cupcakes

Preparation Time: 15 minutes **Cooking Time:** 20-25 minutes **Servings:** 12 cupcakes

Ingredients:
- 2 cups almond flour
- 1/2 cup granulated sugar or sweetener of choice
- 1/4 cup melted butter or coconut oil
- 4 eggs
- 2 tablespoons unsweetened cocoa powder
- 1 tablespoon red food coloring
- 1 teaspoon vanilla extract
- 1 teaspoon baking powder
- Pinch of salt

Directions:
1. Preheat the oven to 350°F (175°C) and line a muffin tin with cupcake liners.
2. In a mixing bowl, combine almond flour, sugar, cocoa powder, baking powder, and salt.
3. In another bowl, whisk together melted butter, eggs, red food coloring, and vanilla extract.
4. Gradually add the wet ingredients to the dry ingredients, mixing until well combined.
5. Pour the batter into the cupcake liners, filling each about two-thirds full.
6. Bake for 20-25 minutes or until a toothpick inserted into the center comes out clean.
7. Let the cupcakes cool in the tin for 5 minutes, then transfer to a wire rack to cool completely.

Recipe Variations:
- Replace part of the almond flour with coconut flour for a slightly lighter texture.
- Incorporate a cream cheese frosting for a classic red velvet cupcake.

Topping Options:
- Frost with cream cheese frosting or a vanilla buttercream.
- Garnish with red sprinkles or a dusting of cocoa powder.

Customization Options:
- Adjust sweetness or experiment with natural food coloring alternatives.

Important Notes:
- Ensure the cupcakes are completely cooled before frosting.

Nutritional Value: (Per Cupcake)
- Calories: ~190
- Total Fat: 15g
- Carbohydrates: 7g
- Fiber: 2g
- Protein: 6g

Almond Flour Blueberry Cupcakes

Preparation Time: 15 minutes **Cooking Time:** 20-25 minutes **Servings:** 12 cupcakes

Ingredients:
- 2 cups almond flour
- 1/2 cup granulated sugar or sweetener of choice
- 1/4 cup melted butter or coconut oil
- 4 eggs
- 1/2 cup fresh blueberries
- 2 teaspoons baking powder
- 1 teaspoon vanilla extract
- Pinch of salt

Directions:
1. Preheat the oven to 350°F (175°C) and line a muffin tin with cupcake liners.
2. In a mixing bowl, combine almond flour, sugar, baking powder, and salt.
3. In another bowl, whisk together melted butter, eggs, and vanilla extract.
4. Gradually add the wet ingredients to the dry ingredients, mixing until well combined.
5. Gently fold in the fresh blueberries into the batter.
6. Pour the batter into the cupcake liners, filling each about two-thirds full.
7. Bake for 20-25 minutes or until a toothpick inserted into the center comes out clean.
8. Let the cupcakes cool in the tin for 5 minutes, then transfer to a wire rack to cool completely.

Recipe Variations:
- Use frozen blueberries if fresh ones are not available.
- Add lemon zest for a blueberry-lemon flavor combination.

Topping Options:
- Frost with a vanilla glaze or a light whipped cream.
- Garnish with additional blueberries or a sprinkle of powdered sugar.

Customization Options:
- Adjust sweetness or add a hint of cinnamon for variation.

Important Notes:
- Ensure the cupcakes are completely cooled before frosting.

Nutritional Value: (Per Cupcake)
- Calories: ~190
- Total Fat: 15g
- Carbohydrates: 7g
- Fiber: 2g
- Protein: 6g

Almond Flour Banana Cupcakes

Preparation Time: 15 minutes **Cooking Time:** 20-25 minutes **Servings:** 12 cupcakes

Ingredients:
- 2 cups almond flour
- 1/2 cup granulated sugar or sweetener of choice
- 1/4 cup melted butter or coconut oil
- 4 ripe bananas, mashed
- 4 eggs
- 1 teaspoon baking powder
- 1 teaspoon vanilla extract
- Pinch of salt

Directions:
1. Preheat the oven to 350°F (175°C) and line a muffin tin with cupcake liners.
2. In a mixing bowl, combine almond flour, sugar, baking powder, and salt.
3. In another bowl, whisk together melted butter, mashed bananas, eggs, and vanilla extract.
4. Gradually add the wet ingredients to the dry ingredients, mixing until well combined.
5. Pour the batter into the cupcake liners, filling each about two-thirds full.
6. Bake for 20-25 minutes or until a toothpick inserted into the center comes out clean.
7. Let the cupcakes cool in the tin for 5 minutes, then transfer to a wire rack to cool completely.

Recipe Variations:
- Add chopped nuts like walnuts or pecans for added texture.
- Incorporate cinnamon or nutmeg for a banana bread-like flavor.

Topping Options:
- Frost with a cream cheese frosting or a caramel drizzle.
- Garnish with banana slices or a sprinkle of cinnamon.

Customization Options:
- Adjust sweetness or experiment with different banana varieties for varied sweetness.

Important Notes:
- Ensure the cupcakes are completely cooled before frosting.

Nutritional Value: (Per Cupcake)
- Calories: ~200
- Total Fat: 16g
- Carbohydrates: 8g
- Fiber: 2g
- Protein: 6g

Almond Flour Strawberry Cupcakes

Preparation Time: 15 minutes **Cooking Time:** 20-25 minutes **Servings:** 12 cupcakes

Ingredients:
- 2 cups almond flour
- 1/2 cup granulated sugar or sweetener of choice
- 1/4 cup melted butter or coconut oil
- 4 eggs
- 1 cup finely chopped fresh strawberries
- 2 teaspoons baking powder
- 1 teaspoon vanilla extract
- Pinch of salt

Directions:
1. Preheat the oven to 350°F (175°C) and line a muffin tin with cupcake liners.
2. In a mixing bowl, combine almond flour, sugar, baking powder, and salt.
3. In another bowl, whisk together melted butter, eggs, and vanilla extract.
4. Gradually add the wet ingredients to the dry ingredients, mixing until well combined.
5. Gently fold in the finely chopped fresh strawberries into the batter.
6. Pour the batter into the cupcake liners, filling each about two-thirds full.
7. Bake for 20-25 minutes or until a toothpick inserted into the center comes out clean.
8. Let the cupcakes cool in the tin for 5 minutes, then transfer to a wire rack to cool completely.

Recipe Variations:
- Use frozen strawberries if fresh ones are not available.
- Add a teaspoon of lemon zest for a strawberry-lemon combination.

Topping Options:
- Frost with a strawberry buttercream or a simple powdered sugar glaze.
- Garnish with a slice of fresh strawberry or a sprinkle of chopped nuts.

Customization Options:
- Adjust sweetness or add a splash of strawberry extract for a more intense flavor.

Important Notes:
- Ensure the cupcakes are completely cooled before frosting.

Nutritional Value: (Per Cupcake)
- Calories: ~200
- Total Fat: 16g
- Carbohydrates: 8g
- Fiber: 2g
- Protein: 6g

ALMOND FLOUR COOKIES

Chewy almond flour cookies are rich and tasty, perfect for a gluten-free snack with milk or tea.

Almond Flour Chocolate Chip Cookies

Preparation Time: 15 minutes **Cooking Time:** 10-12 minutes **Servings:** About 24 cookies

Ingredients:
- 2 cups almond flour
- 1/2 cup melted coconut oil or butter
- 1/2 cup maple syrup or sweetener of choice
- 1 teaspoon vanilla extract
- 1/2 teaspoon baking soda
- 1/4 teaspoon salt
- 1 cup dark chocolate chips

Directions:
1. Preheat the oven to 350°F (175°C) and line a baking sheet with parchment paper.
2. In a bowl, mix almond flour, melted coconut oil, maple syrup, vanilla extract, baking soda, and salt until well combined.
3. Fold in the dark chocolate chips.
4. Scoop tablespoon-sized portions of dough onto the prepared baking sheet, spacing them about 2 inches apart.
5. Flatten each cookie slightly with the back of a spoon or your fingers.
6. Bake for 10-12 minutes or until the edges are golden brown.
7. Allow the cookies to cool on the baking sheet for 5 minutes before transferring them to a wire rack to cool completely.

Recipe Variations:
- Use different types of chocolate chips like milk chocolate or white chocolate.
- Add chopped nuts such as walnuts or pecans for extra crunch.

Customization Options:
- Adjust sweetness by altering the amount of maple syrup.
- Experiment with different extracts like almond or hazelnut for unique flavors.

Important Notes:
- The cookies may seem soft when first out of the oven but will firm up as they cool.

Nutritional Value: (Per Cookie)
- Calories: ~120
- Total Fat: 10g
- Carbohydrates: 7g
- Fiber: 2g
- Protein: 2g

Almond Flour Shortbread Cookies

Preparation Time: 15 minutes **Cooking Time:** 12-15 minutes **Servings:** About 20 cookies

Ingredients:
- 2 cups almond flour
- 1/2 cup melted butter or coconut oil
- 1/4 cup powdered sugar or sweetener of choice
- 1 teaspoon vanilla extract
- Pinch of salt

Directions:
1. Preheat the oven to 325°F (160°C) and line a baking sheet with parchment paper.
2. In a bowl, mix almond flour, melted butter, powdered sugar, vanilla extract, and a pinch of salt until a dough forms.
3. Roll the dough into a log, wrap it in plastic wrap, and refrigerate for at least 30 minutes.
4. Slice the chilled dough into 1/4-inch thick rounds.
5. Place the rounds on the prepared baking sheet.
6. Bake for 12-15 minutes or until the edges are lightly golden.
7. Let the cookies cool on the baking sheet for 5 minutes before transferring them to a wire rack to cool completely.

Recipe Variations:
- Dip cooled cookies in melted chocolate for a chocolate-covered version.
- Add a sprinkle of sea salt on top for a sweet and salty combination.

Customization Options:
- Adjust sweetness by altering the amount of powdered sugar.
- Experiment with different extracts like almond or lemon for varied flavors.

Important Notes:
- These cookies are delicate when warm, so handle with care.

Nutritional Value: (Per Cookie)
- Calories: ~90
- Total Fat: 8g
- Carbohydrates: 3g
- Fiber: 1g
- Protein: 2g

Almond Flour Snickerdoodle Cookies

Preparation Time: 15 minutes **Cooking Time:** 10-12 minutes **Servings:** About 24 cookies

Ingredients:
- 2 cups almond flour
- 1/2 cup melted butter or coconut oil
- 1/3 cup granulated sugar or sweetener of choice
- 1 teaspoon vanilla extract
- 1/2 teaspoon cream of tartar
- 1/2 teaspoon baking soda
- 1/4 teaspoon salt

For Rolling:
- 2 tablespoons granulated sugar
- 1 teaspoon ground cinnamon

Directions:
1. Preheat the oven to 350°F (175°C) and line a baking sheet with parchment paper.
2. In a bowl, mix almond flour, melted butter, granulated sugar, vanilla extract, cream of tartar, baking soda, and salt until well combined.
3. In a separate small bowl, combine sugar and ground cinnamon for rolling.
4. Scoop tablespoon-sized portions of cookie dough and roll them into balls.
5. Roll each ball in the sugar-cinnamon mixture to coat.
6. Place the coated balls on the prepared baking sheet, spacing them about 2 inches apart.
7. Flatten each cookie slightly with the back of a spoon or your fingers.
8. Bake for 10-12 minutes or until the edges are golden brown.
9. Allow the cookies to cool on the baking sheet for 5 minutes before transferring them to a wire rack to cool completely.

Recipe Variations:
- Add a pinch of nutmeg for a spiced variation.
- Incorporate finely chopped nuts for added texture.

Customization Options:
- Adjust sweetness by altering the amount of granulated sugar.
- Experiment with different ratios of cinnamon for varied spice levels.

Important Notes:
- The cookies may seem soft when first out of the oven but will firm up as they cool.

Nutritional Value: (Per Cookie)
- Calories: ~90
- Total Fat: 7g
- Carbohydrates: 4g
- Fiber: 1g
- Protein: 2g

Almond Flour Peanut Butter Cookies

Preparation Time: 15 minutes **Cooking Time:** 10-12 minutes **Servings:** About 18 cookies

Ingredients:
- 2 cups almond flour
- 1/2 cup creamy peanut butter
- 1/2 cup melted butter or coconut oil
- 1/2 cup granulated sugar or sweetener of choice
- 1 teaspoon vanilla extract
- 1/2 teaspoon baking soda
- 1/4 teaspoon salt

Directions:
1. Preheat the oven to 350°F (175°C) and line a baking sheet with parchment paper.
2. In a bowl, mix almond flour, peanut butter, melted butter, granulated sugar, vanilla extract, baking soda, and salt until well combined.
3. Scoop tablespoon-sized portions of cookie dough onto the prepared baking sheet, spacing them about 2 inches apart.
4. Flatten each cookie slightly with the back of a spoon or your fingers.
5. Bake for 10-12 minutes or until the edges are lightly golden.
6. Allow the cookies to cool on the baking sheet for 5 minutes before transferring them to a wire rack to cool completely.

Recipe Variations:
- Fold in chopped peanuts for added crunch.
- Drizzle melted chocolate on top for a peanut butter-chocolate twist.

Customization Options:
- Adjust sweetness by altering the amount of granulated sugar.
- Experiment with different nut butters for unique flavors.

Important Notes:
- These cookies are delicate when warm, so handle them gently until cooled.

Nutritional Value: (Per Cookie)
- Calories: ~120
- Total Fat: 10g
- Carbohydrates: 6g
- Fiber: 1g
- Protein: 3g

Almond Flour Coconut Macaroons

Preparation Time: 15 minutes **Cooking Time:** 15-20 minutes **Servings:** About 18 cookies

Ingredients:
- 2 cups almond flour
- 2 cups shredded unsweetened coconut
- 1/2 cup maple syrup or sweetener of choice
- 1/4 cup melted coconut oil
- 1 teaspoon vanilla extract
- Pinch of salt

Directions:
1. Preheat the oven to 325°F (160°C) and line a baking sheet with parchment paper.
2. In a bowl, combine almond flour, shredded coconut, maple syrup, melted coconut oil, vanilla extract, and a pinch of salt. Mix until well combined.
3. Scoop tablespoon-sized portions of the mixture onto the prepared baking sheet, forming mounds.
4. Bake for 15-20 minutes or until the macaroons are lightly golden on the edges.
5. Let the macaroons cool on the baking sheet for 5 minutes before transferring them to a wire rack to cool completely.

Recipe Variations:
- Dip the cooled macaroons in melted chocolate for an added layer of flavor.
- Add a teaspoon of almond extract for an almond-coconut combination.

Customization Options:
- Adjust sweetness by altering the amount of maple syrup.
- Experiment with different types of shredded coconut for varied textures.

Important Notes:
- Ensure the macaroons are completely cooled before storing.

Nutritional Value: (Per Macaroon)
- Calories: ~110
- Total Fat: 9g
- Carbohydrates: 5g
- Fiber: 2g
- Protein: 2g

Almond Flour Thumbprint Cookies

Preparation Time: 15 minutes **Cooking Time:** 12-15 minutes **Servings:** About 20 cookies

Ingredients:
- 2 cups almond flour
- 1/4 cup melted butter or coconut oil
- 1/4 cup maple syrup or sweetener of choice
- 1 teaspoon vanilla extract
- 1/4 cup fruit preserves or jam of choice

Directions:
1. Preheat the oven to 350°F (175°C) and line a baking sheet with parchment paper.
2. In a bowl, mix almond flour, melted butter, maple syrup, and vanilla extract until a dough forms.
3. Roll tablespoon-sized portions of the dough into balls and place them on the prepared baking sheet.
4. Create an indentation in the center of each cookie using your thumb or the back of a spoon.
5. Fill each indentation with a small amount of fruit preserves or jam.
6. Bake for 12-15 minutes or until the edges of the cookies are lightly golden.
7. Allow the cookies to cool on the baking sheet for 5 minutes before transferring them to a wire rack to cool completely.

Recipe Variations:
- Use various flavors of jam or preserves for different tastes.
- Dust the cooled cookies with powdered sugar for a decorative touch.

Customization Options:
- Adjust sweetness by altering the amount of maple syrup.
- Experiment with different types of preserves or fillings for variety.

Important Notes:
- Handle the cookies carefully when filling to prevent crumbling.

Nutritional Value: (Per Cookie)
- Calories: ~90
- Total Fat: 7g
- Carbohydrates: 5g
- Fiber: 1g
- Protein: 2g

Almond Flour Oatmeal Cookies

Preparation Time: 15 minutes **Cooking Time:** 10-12 minutes **Servings:** About 24 cookies

Ingredients:
- 1 1/2 cups almond flour
- 1 1/2 cups rolled oats
- 1/2 cup melted butter or coconut oil
- 1/2 cup maple syrup or sweetener of choice
- 1 teaspoon vanilla extract
- 1/2 teaspoon baking soda
- 1/4 teaspoon cinnamon
- Pinch of salt

Directions:
1. Preheat the oven to 350°F (175°C) and line a baking sheet with parchment paper.
2. In a bowl, mix almond flour, rolled oats, melted butter, maple syrup, vanilla extract, baking soda, cinnamon, and a pinch of salt until well combined.
3. Scoop tablespoon-sized portions of the dough onto the prepared baking sheet, spacing them about 2 inches apart.
4. Flatten each cookie slightly with the back of a spoon or your fingers.
5. Bake for 10-12 minutes or until the edges are lightly golden.
6. Allow the cookies to cool on the baking sheet for 5 minutes before transferring them to a wire rack to cool completely.

Recipe Variations:
- Add raisins, chocolate chips, or chopped nuts for extra texture.
- Incorporate a dash of nutmeg or allspice for additional flavor.

Customization Options:
- Adjust sweetness by altering the amount of maple syrup.
- Experiment with different types of oats for varied textures.

Important Notes:
- These cookies will firm up as they cool.

Nutritional Value: (Per Cookie)
- Calories: ~90
- Total Fat: 7g
- Carbohydrates: 6g
- Fiber: 1g
- Protein: 2g

Almond Flour Ginger Cookies

Preparation Time: 15 minutes **Cooking Time:** 10-12 minutes **Servings:** About 24 cookies

Ingredients:
- 2 cups almond flour
- 1/4 cup melted butter or coconut oil
- 1/2 cup molasses
- 1/4 cup granulated sugar or sweetener of choice
- 1 teaspoon ground ginger
- 1/2 teaspoon ground cinnamon
- 1/4 teaspoon ground cloves
- 1/2 teaspoon baking soda
- Pinch of salt

Directions:
1. Preheat the oven to 350°F (175°C) and line a baking sheet with parchment paper.
2. In a bowl, mix almond flour, melted butter, molasses, granulated sugar, ground ginger, ground cinnamon, ground cloves, baking soda, and a pinch of salt until well combined.
3. Scoop tablespoon-sized portions of the dough onto the prepared baking sheet, spacing them about 2 inches apart.
4. Flatten each cookie slightly with the back of a spoon or your fingers.
5. Bake for 10-12 minutes or until the edges are lightly golden.
6. Allow the cookies to cool on the baking sheet for 5 minutes before transferring them to a wire rack to cool completely.

Recipe Variations:
- Add a dash of black pepper for a hint of spiciness.
- Dust the cooled cookies with powdered sugar for a decorative finish.

Customization Options:
- Adjust sweetness by altering the amount of granulated sugar or molasses.
- Experiment with different spice combinations for varied flavors.

Important Notes:
- These cookies will become firmer as they cool.

Nutritional Value: (Per Cookie)
- Calories: ~90
- Total Fat: 7g
- Carbohydrates: 6g
- Fiber: 1g
- Protein: 2g

ALMOND FLOUR BARS

Almond flour-based bars are nutty and decadent. They're a guilt-free option for snacking or dessert.

Almond Flour Blondies

Preparation Time: 15 minutes **Cooking Time**: 20-25 minutes **Servings**: 16 blondies

Ingredients:
- 2 cups almond flour
- 1/2 cup melted butter or coconut oil
- 1/2 cup brown sugar or sweetener of choice
- 2 eggs
- 1 teaspoon vanilla extract
- 1/4 teaspoon baking soda
- Pinch of salt
- 1/2 cup chocolate chips or chopped nuts (optional)

Directions:
1. Preheat the oven to 350°F (175°C) and line an 8x8-inch baking pan with parchment paper.
2. In a bowl, mix melted butter, brown sugar, eggs, and vanilla extract until well combined.
3. Add almond flour, baking soda, and a pinch of salt. Mix until a smooth batter forms.
4. Fold in chocolate chips or chopped nuts if desired.
5. Spread the batter evenly into the prepared baking pan.
6. Bake for 20-25 minutes or until the edges are golden and a toothpick inserted into the center comes out clean.
7. Let the blondies cool completely in the pan before slicing.

Recipe Variations:
- Add butterscotch chips or shredded coconut for a twist.
- Incorporate dried fruits like cranberries or apricots for added texture.

Topping Options:
- Drizzle melted chocolate on top for extra sweetness.
- Dust with powdered sugar before serving.

Customization Options:
- Adjust sweetness by altering the amount of sugar used.
- Experiment with different types of nuts or chocolate for variety.

Important Notes:
- Allow the blondies to cool completely to achieve the best texture.

Nutritional Value: (Per Blondie)
- Calories: ~160
- Total Fat: 13g
- Carbohydrates: 8g
- Fiber: 2g
- Protein: 4g

Almond Flour Brownies

Preparation Time: 15 minutes **Cooking Time:** 25-30 minutes **Servings:** 16 brownies

Ingredients:
- 2 cups almond flour
- 1/2 cup melted butter or coconut oil
- 1/2 cup unsweetened cocoa powder
- 1 cup granulated sugar or sweetener of choice
- 3 eggs
- 1 teaspoon vanilla extract
- 1/4 teaspoon baking soda
- Pinch of salt
- 1/2 cup chocolate chips or chopped nuts (optional)

Directions:
1. Preheat the oven to 350°F (175°C) and line an 8x8-inch baking pan with parchment paper.
2. In a bowl, mix melted butter, cocoa powder, granulated sugar, eggs, and vanilla extract until well combined.
3. Add almond flour, baking soda, and a pinch of salt. Mix until a smooth batter forms.
4. Fold in chocolate chips or chopped nuts if desired.
5. Spread the batter evenly into the prepared baking pan.
6. Bake for 25-30 minutes or until a toothpick inserted into the center comes out with a few moist crumbs.
7. Allow the brownies to cool completely in the pan before cutting into squares.

Recipe Variations:
- Swirl in peanut butter or caramel for added richness.
- Add a sprinkle of sea salt on top for a sweet-salty contrast.

Topping Options:
- Top with a layer of ganache or frosting for extra indulgence.
- Garnish with a dusting of cocoa powder before serving.

Customization Options:
- Adjust sweetness by altering the amount of sugar used.
- Experiment with different types of chocolate or nuts for varied flavors.

Important Notes:
- Ensure the brownies are completely cooled before slicing for clean cuts.

Nutritional Value: (Per Brownie)
- Calories: ~180
- Total Fat: 14g
- Carbohydrates: 12g
- Fiber: 2g
- Protein: 4g

Almond Flour Lemon Bars

Preparation Time: 20 minutes **Cooking Time**: 25-30 minutes **Chilling Time**: 2 hours **Servings**: 16 bars

Ingredients:
- For the Crust:
  - 2 cups almond flour
  - 1/4 cup melted butter or coconut oil
  - 2 tablespoons granulated sugar or sweetener of choice
  - Pinch of salt
- For the Lemon Filling:
  - 4 large eggs
  - 3/4 cup freshly squeezed lemon juice
  - 1 cup granulated sugar or sweetener of choice
  - 1/4 cup almond flour
- Zest from 2 lemons
- Powdered sugar for dusting (optional)

Directions:
1. Preheat the oven to 350°F (175°C) and line an 8x8-inch baking pan with parchment paper.
2. In a bowl, mix almond flour, melted butter, granulated sugar, and a pinch of salt for the crust.
3. Press the mixture evenly into the bottom of the prepared baking pan.
4. Bake the crust for 12-15 minutes or until lightly golden. Remove from the oven and let it cool slightly.
5. In another bowl, whisk together eggs, lemon juice, granulated sugar, almond flour, and lemon zest for the filling.
6. Pour the filling over the baked crust.
7. Bake for 25-30 minutes or until the filling is set.
8. Allow the bars to cool completely at room temperature, then refrigerate for at least 2 hours before slicing.
9. Dust with powdered sugar before serving if desired.

Recipe Variations:
- Add a tablespoon of cornstarch for a thicker lemon layer.
- Incorporate a few drops of yellow food coloring for a brighter appearance.

Topping Options:
- Dust with additional lemon zest for a burst of citrus flavor.
- Serve with a dollop of whipped cream or a scoop of vanilla ice cream.

Customization Options:
- Adjust sweetness by altering the amount of sugar used.
- Experiment with lime or orange juice for different citrus variations.

Important Notes:
- Chill the bars thoroughly for easier slicing and serving.

Nutritional Value: (Per Bar)
- Calories: ~160
- Total Fat: 11g
- Carbohydrates: 13g
- Fiber: 2g
- Protein: 4g

Almond Flour Raspberry Bars

Preparation Time: 20 minutes **Cooking Time:** 25-30 minutes **Chilling Time:** 2 hours **Servings:** 16 bars

Ingredients:
- For the Crust:
  - 2 cups almond flour
  - 1/4 cup melted butter or coconut oil
  - 2 tablespoons granulated sugar or sweetener of choice
  - Pinch of salt
- For the Raspberry Filling:
  - 2 cups fresh raspberries
  - 1/4 cup granulated sugar or sweetener of choice
  - 1 tablespoon lemon juice
  - 2 tablespoons almond flour

Directions:

1. Preheat the oven to 350°F (175°C) and line an 8x8-inch baking pan with parchment paper.
2. In a bowl, mix almond flour, melted butter, granulated sugar, and a pinch of salt for the crust.
3. Press the mixture evenly into the bottom of the prepared baking pan.
4. Bake the crust for 12-15 minutes or until lightly golden. Remove from the oven and let it cool slightly.
5. In a saucepan, combine raspberries, granulated sugar, and lemon juice over medium heat.
6. Cook and stir until the raspberries break down and the mixture thickens slightly, about 5-7 minutes.
7. Remove the raspberry mixture from heat and stir in almond flour.
8. Spread the raspberry filling over the baked crust.
9. Bake for 25-30 minutes or until the filling is set.
10. Allow the bars to cool completely at room temperature, then refrigerate for at least 2 hours before slicing.

Recipe Variations:
- Add a teaspoon of vanilla extract to the raspberry filling for extra flavor.
- Mix in a tablespoon of chia seeds to the filling for added texture.

Topping Options:
- Dust with powdered sugar before serving for a decorative touch.
- Serve with a dollop of whipped cream or a scoop of vanilla ice cream.

Customization Options:
- Adjust sweetness by altering the amount of sugar used in the filling.
- Experiment with other berries or a mix of berries for different flavors.

Important Notes:
- Chill the bars thoroughly for easier slicing and serving.

Nutritional Value: (Per Bar)
- Calories: ~150
- Total Fat: 11g
- Carbohydrates: 11g
- Fiber: 3g
- Protein: 4g